IN NO TIME

Access
2000

IN NO TIME

Access
2000

Ignatz Schels

Prentice
Hall

AN IMPRINT OF PEARSON EDUCATION

PEARSON EDUCATION LIMITED

Head Office:
Edinburgh Gate
Harlow CM20 2JE
Tel: +44 (0)1279 623623
Fax: +44 (0)1279 431059

London Office:
128 Long Acre
London WC2E 9AN
Tel: +44 (0)207 447 2000
Fax: +44 (0)207 240 5771

First published in Great Britain in 2000

© Pearson Education Limited 2000

First published in 1999 as *Access 2000: leicht, klar, sofort*
by Markt & Technik Buch- und Software-Verlag GmbH
Martin-Kollar-Straße 10–12
D-81829 Munich
GERMANY

Library of Congress Cataloging in Publication Data
Available from the publisher.

British Library Cataloguing in Publication Data
A CIP catalogue record for this book can be obtained from the British Library.

ISBN 0-13-086445-5

10 9 8 7 6 5 4 3 2 1

Translated and typeset by Cybertechnics, Sheffield.
Printed and bound in Great Britain by Henry Ling Ltd, at The Dorset Press, Dorchester, Dorset.

The publishers' policy is to use paper manufactured from sustainable forests.

Contents

1   **Database basics**   8

2   **Workshop: Office management**   42

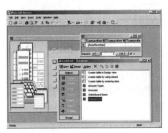

6 A personal birthdays database 186

7 The Shareware Archive 222

8 Vacation offers and bookings 260

9 Invoices 290

Help 316

Appendix 330

Index 341

Dear Reader,

So you are determined to learn how to work with the database program Access 2000. Let me first tell you that I am very happy you have decided to use my book for this purpose. I am sure you will not regret this decision. In the many years I have worked as an EDP teacher, I have always had the same experience: software is developed by programmers, and programmers often think that the user knows as much as they do about programming and computers. Correspondingly, forms, manuals, and on-screen help texts are very difficult to understand and work with.

With this book, I want to prove to you that it is possible to do things differently. The most important parts of the program will be explained to you in an easy way, connections are pointed out whenever necessary, terminology is explained, and the step-by-step instructions will lead you to quick results and success.

What do I ask of you? You should be reasonably familiar with the Windows operating system. Apart from that, you need nothing else but enjoy your work, and have a good deal of curiosity and thirst for action. Of course you also need a slice of patience, if things should not work out as they ought to, and a dash of humour which you should not lose in any situation. If you are equipped with all these things, you have what it takes and you can start working with Access 2000.

I hope you are going to enjoy working with your program and your IN NO TIME book.

Ignatz Schels

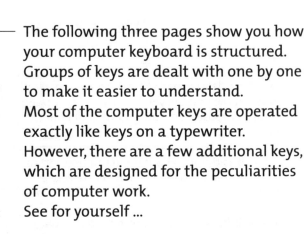

The following three pages show you how
your computer keyboard is structured.
Groups of keys are dealt with one by one
to make it easier to understand.
Most of the computer keys are operated
exactly like keys on a typewriter.
However, there are a few additional keys,
which are designed for the peculiarities
of computer work.
See for yourself ...

Typewriter keys

Use these keys exactly as you do on a typewriter.
The Enter key is also used to send commands to your computer.

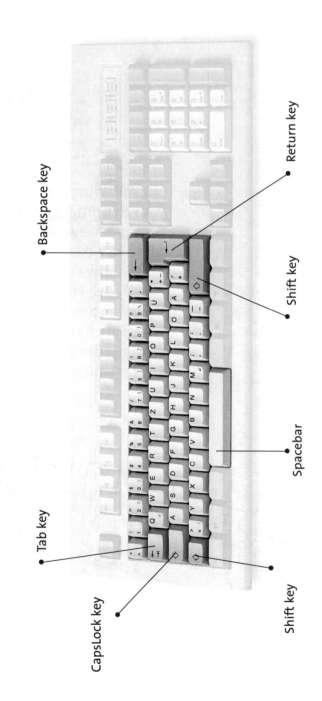

Backspace key

Return key

Shift key

Tab key

Spacebar

CapsLock key

Shift key

Special keys, function keys, status lights, numeric key pad

Special keys and function keys are used for special tasks in computer operation. The Ctrl, Alt and AltGr keys are usually used in combination with other keys. The Esc key can cancel commands. Insert and Delete can be used, amongst other things, to insert and delete text.

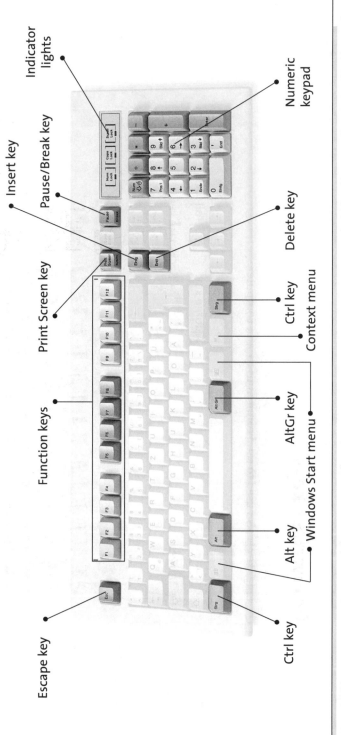

Escape key

Function keys

Print Screen key

Pause/Break key

Insert key

Indicator lights

Numeric keypad

Delete key

Ctrl key

Context menu

AltGr key

Windows Start menu

Alt key

Ctrl key

Navigation keys

These keys are used to move around the screen.

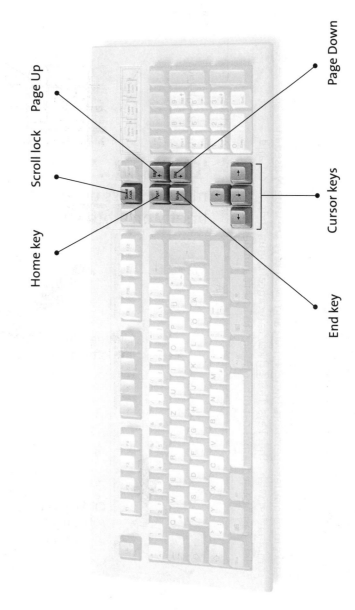

Page Up

Scroll lock

Home key

Page Down

Cursor keys

End key

'Click on ...'

means: press once
briefly on a button.

Clicking with
the left mouse
button ...

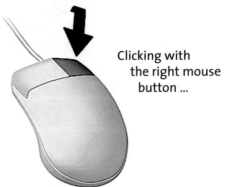

Clicking with
the right mouse
button ...

'Double-click on ...'

means: press the left button
twice briefly in quick
succession

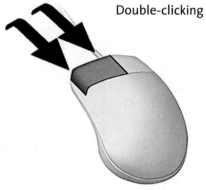

Double-clicking

'Drag ...'

means: click on an object with the left
mouse button, keep the button
pressed, move the mouse and thus
drag the item to another position.

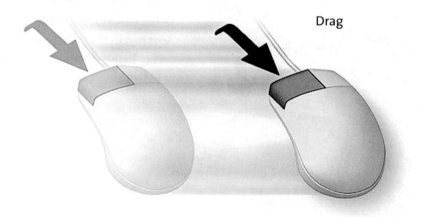

Drag

What's in this chapter:

What is a database? How do you create and open a database? What does a database consist of? This chapter will answer these and other questions about databases in general. After reading it, you will be able to work with existing databases. However, at the same time, you will learn how to create databases with Access 2000. Have a look at an example of a professional database with all its modules and links.

You are going to learn about:

Basic knowledge

Before you start working with Access 2000, you should familiarise yourself with a few items of database terminology. First we are going to introduce the two terms database and database management system (DBMS):

A **database** is a collection of data, for example in the form of tables. Relational databases use linked tables.

A **database management system (DBMS)** is used for recording, storing, maintenance, and management of a database. Access 2000 is a DBMS with which to create new databases and manage existing databases.

The core of every database is the table, in which data is stored. With the database management system you record data and link data from different tables into a relational system.

A **table** is divided into data fields and data records. The columns are referred to as fields and the rows as records. The field names, which are listed in the first row, are used to refer to the fields.

Here is a small table with five columns and four rows or, in database terminology, five fields and four data records:

First Name	Name	Street	Postcode	City
Paul	Jones	12 Otley Road	LS0 1ZX	Leeds
Shirley	Smith	33b Norwood Place	SW0 1XY	London
Albert	Edwards	15 York Road	OL3 1PP	Oldham

To ensure that the fields in a table cannot be filled with just any data, so-called field properties are set up via the DBMS. A property of the field 'Name', for example, could be the field length (e.g. greater than 0 [zero] letters or limited to 20 letters). If you want to restrict the 'Postcode' field to 9 digits, you must change the 'Postcode' field properties accordingly.

WHAT'S THIS?

The **field properties** determine rules for the contents of the field. These rules must be complied with when entering data.

Access 2000 databases are relational. This means that the tables are linked to each other. When planning databases, it is particularly important to define these links in advance. The more elaborate the links, the easier it is to analyse the data later on.

WHAT'S THIS?

Tables in **relational** databases are linked. In this way, it is possible to extract data, which share a code, from several databases.

To illustrate this relativity with a simple example, we assume that you are planning to create a products database. The table could look like this:

Product Number	Product Name	Price	Manufacturer
1001	Screwdriver	10.95	Smith Ltd
1002	Spirit level	4.95	Harper Co.
...			

You will require a second table, which contains the manufacturer's data:

Manufacturer Number	Manufacturer	City	Phone Number
1001	Smith Ltd	Leeds	(0113) 123 456
1002	Harper Co.	Oldham	(01457) 123 456

This distribution would be a little awkward. What happens if the manufacturer of a product changes? How can you find all the products by manufacturers from a particular region? Database analyses of this type should be considered, when creating a database. A relational link between the two tables is recommended. Create the first table in a different way: instead of the manufacturer's name, simply store its number.

Product Number	Product Name	Price	Manufacturer
1001	Screwdriver	10.95	1001
1002	Spirit level	4.95	1002

Later you will link the two tables, which will then enable you to extract specific data from both tables by means of queries.

Product Name	Product Number
Screwdriver	1001
Spirit level	1002

Relational Link

Manufacturer Number	Manufacturer	City
1001	Smith Ltd	Leeds
1002	Harper Co.	Oldham

Product Name	Manufacturer	City
Screwdriver	Smith Ltd	Leeds
Spirit level	Harper Co.	Oldham

Starting Access 2000

Enough about theory. Start your program and let the book help you acquaint yourself with common database techniques.

The Standard Office package has Word, Excel, PowerPoint and Outlook. The Professional Version also contains Access 2000.

Access 2000 has already been installed on your hard disk – that is our starting point. If you only have the program on CD-ROM (in the Office Professional package), you need to install it onto your hard disk using its installation program.

After switching on your computer, if this is networked, you are probably prompted to type in your password and username.

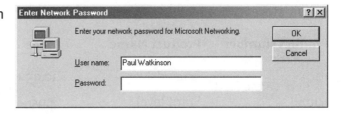

As soon as you have entered both details, the desktop is displayed.

This is the electronic desk on which you can find the symbols for starting programs.

At the right-hand edge of the screen, you can see the so-called shortcut bar, which also offers symbols. You can start a specific program by simply clicking on the corresponding symbol. In this picture the bar already contains a symbol for Access.

At the bottom of your screen, the Taskbar is displayed. With this bar you can activate all programs currently available on your computer. You can quickly switch to a task by clicking on the corresponding button. In the bottom left-hand corner, you will find the Start menu for you to click on.

Let's find out how you start and exit Access 2000.

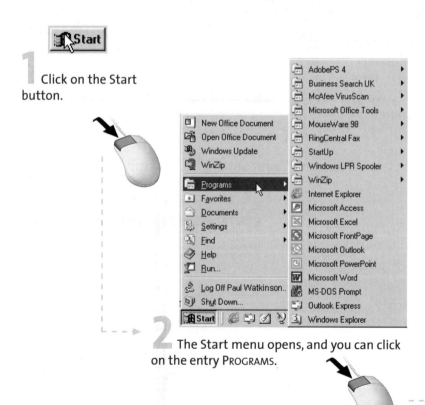

Click on the Start button.

The Start menu opens, and you can click on the entry Programs.

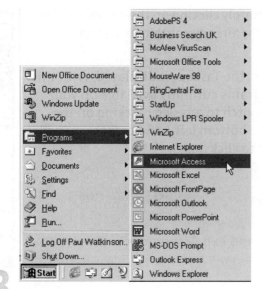

Another menu opens. Choose the MICROSOFT ACCESS menu option.

Access 2000 starts. The program covers the desktop and displays a dialog box. Click on *Cancel* to close it.

15

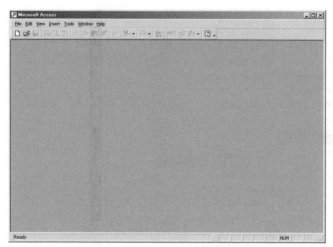

5 Now all you see is the program window with the Title bar, the Menu bar, and a Toolbar.

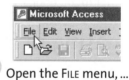

6 Open the FILE menu, ...

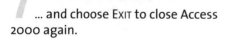

7 ... and choose EXIT to close Access 2000 again.

8 The desktop is displayed, and the Access 2000 symbol disappears from the Task bar.

Navigating in folders and drives

When you are storing data on your computer, you do not simply fill it up until it is full. The computer, or to be precise the data carrier of the computer, is divided into folders. Before we create and store data with our database program, we should take a closer look at the folder structure.

These basic terms should be familiar to you:

A **drive** is the data carrier on which data is stored. In practice this is almost always a hard drive. If you are networked, this drive may even be located on a completely different computer. A drive letter from A to Z is assigned to each drive. C usually refers to the hard drive.

WHAT'S THIS?

A drive is divided into **folders** (formerly: directories). The main folder on the top level contains the subfolders and also files. Often the path, that is, the way to a folder, is stated by listing the individual folders separated by backward slashes: C:\Programs\My Documents\...

Everything stored on a data carrier is a **file**. This file is marked with a file name and a file extension. The name, including the names of the drive and folders (path), may consist of up to 255 characters. The file extension consists of 3 characters. Each folder in the folder structure may contain any number of files.

The best way to learn how to handle drives, folders, and files is by using the Windows Explorer. This is a program which is supplied together with Windows. It not only allows you to display a file, but also to copy, move, or delete it. Deleting files will be necessary as soon

as your drive is too full to record further data.

How are Access 2000 databases stored on the hard drive?
The manufacturer has thought of a very simple principle: everything you put into a database is stored in a single file with the file extension **MDB** for Microsoft DataBase. This database file can store up to 1 gbyte

(=1,000 mbytes) of data. Should that not be enough, you can link external data to the file and thus create a database of practically unlimited size.

Where are databases stored on the hard disk? You decide that – the program Access 2000 does not dictate either in which drive or in which folder databases are placed. However, you are recommended – not only for Access 2000 – to have a specific folder for all data produced by the program. First, this makes it easier to find your data, and second, copying or moving data between databases is easier if the files are close to each other.

It is easy to decide which folder should be allocated to your database files. It is just as easy to create a new folder and declare it to be the new *default database folder*. We will create a new folder with the name *Access in No Time* for the exercises in this book and set up Access 2000 in such a way that all data is searched for and filed in this new folder.

1 Start Windows Explorer with the Start menu.

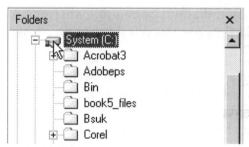

2 Mark the first level of the folder structure by clicking on the drive symbol of the hard disk.

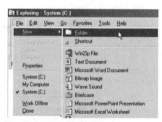

3 Create a new folder with FILE, NEW.

Name	Size	Type	Modified
Access in No Time		File Folder	26/07/99 5:01 PM

4 Enter the folder name 'Access in No Time', and press the Enter key to finish.

5 Now you can start Access 2000 from the Start menu or with the shortcut bar.

6 In the dialog box, which appears after start-up, choose *Blank Access Database*.

7 You now have to name the new database.
Access 2000 switches to the default database folder.

8 When you open this list, you
can see on which level of the folder
structure this folder is located.

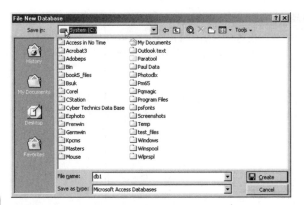

9 Switch back to the main level by clicking on the drive symbol.

10 You can switch to the newly created folder by double-clicking.

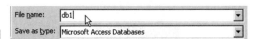

11 Enter the name of the first database (place the cursor into the File Name box by clicking in it), ...

12 ... and complete the new database by clicking on the *Create* button.

23

For the time being, this folder remains your work folder. The new database you have created is automatically saved in this folder, and every time you open a database, the contents of this folder will be shown to you first.

To ensure that, in future, all your database data always end up in this folder, you should set it up as your *default database folder*.

1 Your database is still active. Open the TOOLS menu, ...

2 ... and choose the OPTIONS command.

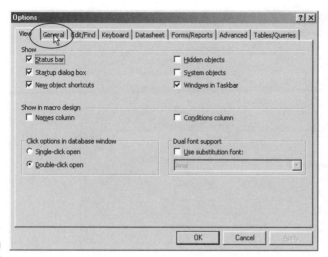

3 A dialog box containing eight tabs opens. Activate the *General* tab by clicking on it with the mouse.

Default database folder:

C:\My Documents\

4 The Default database folder box displays the path that leads to the folder containing the Access 2000 data. Place the cursor in the box.

Default database folder:

C:\Access in No Time

5 Drag the mouse across all the characters, and then overtype them with your folder name.

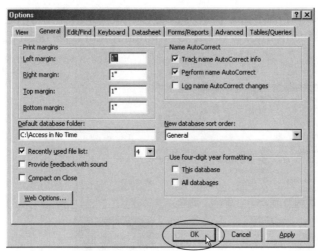

6 This is now your new default database folder.
Confirm your entry by clicking on the *OK* button.

To test the new setting, terminate Access 2000 with Exit from the
File menu and immediately restart the program. When you choose
the first option to create a new database or the *Open an existing
database* option, you will automatically see the contents of your
default database folder.

Example: the 'Northwind' database

Designing databases is not easy. People who – professionally or
privately – work with databases need to spend a lot of time thinking
about database design and must acquire much basic theoretical
knowledge before they can implement their databases. Microsoft,
who designed Access 2000, is of course aware of this problem and
does everything to ease your way into the subject. After all, you are
much-valued customers.

How do you set up a database? It is best to explain this with the example
of a professional database, and this database is supplied with Access

2000. The *Northwind.mdb* database is an example solution, in which the most important techniques of database management have been put into practice.

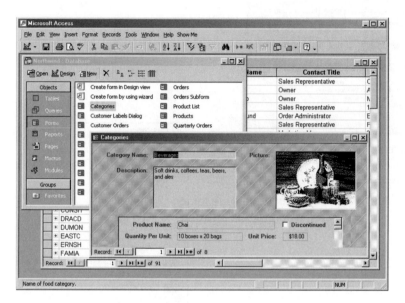

The (fictitious) company 'Northwind Traders' imports and exports delicacies from around the world. The following data is managed in the database:

➡ the company's product data

➡ an index of all suppliers with addresses, phone numbers, and Internet addresses

➡ names and addresses of the sales personnel with details about their education and photographs

➡ a list of all transport companies which can be commissioned for import and export

➡ the orders which have been taken for the products, including order date, method of transport, and shipping costs

Take a look at the example database. It was placed in the Office example folder after Access 2000 was installed on your system:

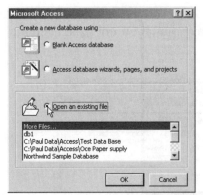

1 Start Access 2000. In the first dialog box, choose *Open an existing database*, or if the program window is already open, the FILE/OPEN menu command.

2 On your hard disk look for the *Programs\Microsoft Office\Office\Samples* folder.

3 Start the *Northwind.mdb* database by double-clicking on the file name.

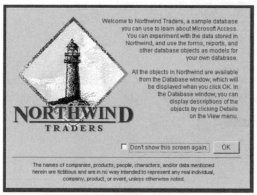

4 The database opens. An entry message tells you about the example.

5 Tick this option by clicking on the check box, so that the message will not be displayed every time you open the database.

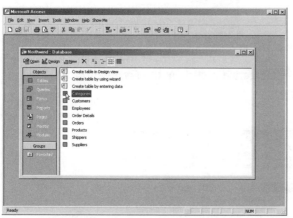

6 The first and most important thing you see in the database is the Database window. Here all the elements of the database are listed. Switch to the Table module, if not already shown, and open the first table by double-clicking on it.

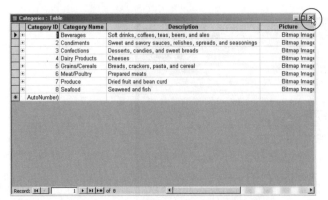

	Category ID	Category Name	Description	Picture
▶ +	1	Beverages	Soft drinks, coffees, teas, beers, and ales	Bitmap Image
+	2	Condiments	Sweet and savory sauces, relishes, spreads, and seasonings	Bitmap Image
+	3	Confections	Desserts, candies, and sweet breads	Bitmap Image
+	4	Dairy Products	Cheeses	Bitmap Image
+	5	Grains/Cereals	Breads, crackers, pasta, and cereal	Bitmap Image
+	6	Meat/Poultry	Prepared meats	Bitmap Image
+	7	Produce	Dried fruit and bean curd	Bitmap Image
+	8	Seafood	Seaweed and fish	Bitmap Image
*	(AutoNumber)			

Record: I◀ ◀ 1 ▶ ▶I ▶* of 8

7 The new window shows the data records of the table. You can close it by clicking on the cross symbol on the Title bar in the top right corner.

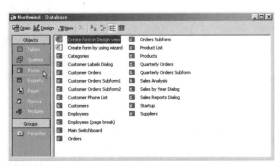

8 Take a look at the forms: on the left on the Objects bar, click on the *Forms* entry, ...

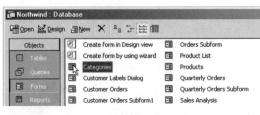

9 ... and open the form with which the previously shown Products table is managed.

10 The form opens. With it, you can modify data from the Products table, or add new products. More about that later on. Now close the form again.

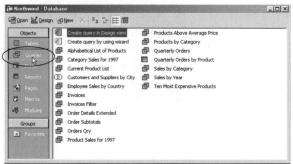

11 In the next module you will find *queries*. Queries are tables which show what is output, and in which form, from individual databases. For example, you can filter data records from tables, or sort them any way you like.

31

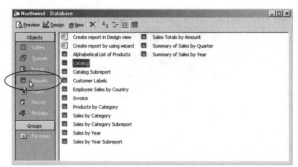

12 With reports, data records from tables and queries are made ready for printing and are then printed out. The appearance of reports can vary significantly – even invoices can be written as reports.

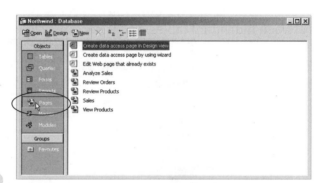

13 In the *Pages* module you can find Wizards which help you create and edit Internet or intranet pages in HTML format.

In the *Macros* module you can find a few further entries. This is where macros – small programs within the program – are stored. A macro contains a collection of instructions that are carried out when the macro is called up (for example, opening a form, entering a date, producing a report, and so on).

The last module with the name *Modules* is reserved for real programs. These programs are written in the Visual Basic for Applications programming language (VBA). VBA programs control professional databases, provide dialogs with the user, and offer many options for exporting and importing and cooperating with the operating system. VBA is often referred to as a developing environment.

Important connections

As in real life, in a database too, good connections are important. Individual database tables need to be linked relationally if they are related (as already mentioned in the section on database basics). The product table, for example, is connected to the supplier table, because in the former only suppliers' numbers are stored, whereas the latter contains all additional suppliers' data.

In the Relationships window you can check the links that exist between individual tables, and if necessary link tables:

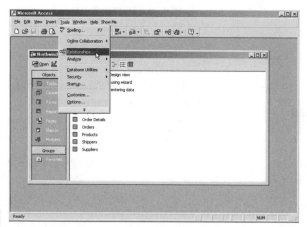

Open the Tools menu, and choose the Relationships entry.

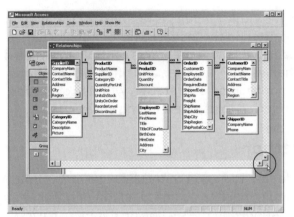

2 To enlarge the window, click on its bottom right-hand corner, and holding down the left mouse button, drag the window frame until it reaches the right size.

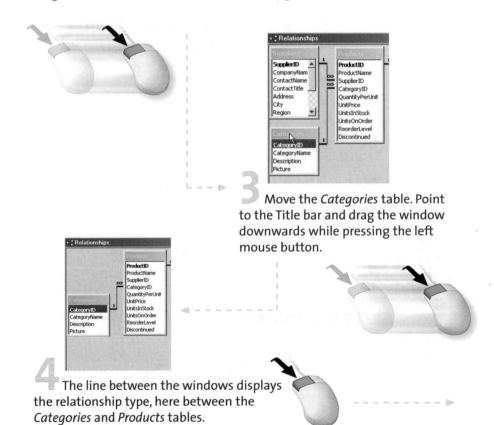

3 Move the *Categories* table. Point to the Title bar and drag the window downwards while pressing the left mouse button.

4 The line between the windows displays the relationship type, here between the *Categories* and *Products* tables.

5 Double-clicking on the line opens a window which details the relationship.

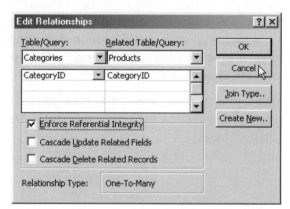

6 Here you can see the fields which link the two tables. Cancel the information without changing anything.

7 Close the Relationships window, too. Reply with *No* to the question whether you want to save formatting changes.

Design mode and Data Sheet View

Every object in a database, whether it is a table, a form, or a report, can be used in two ways by users: they can create, modify, or design it; or work with the object, or collect or print out data. This strict separation of work is supported in Access 2000 by the option of displaying the object either in *Design View* or in *Data Sheet View* or *Form View*.

For example, if you want to add a column to a table, you will open the object in Design View. However, to add new customers to the customer table, you will open it in Data Sheet View. To correct a form where the heading is too small, you need to choose the Design View. To display or process data records field by field you need to switch to Form or Data Sheet View.

Let's have a look at these views and how you can switch between the processing levels in the Customer table of the *Northwind.mdb* example database:

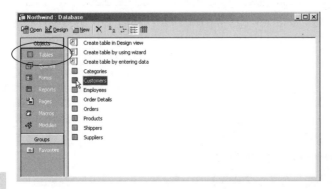

1 In the objects window, activate the Table module, and select the *Customers* table (by clicking on it).

2 In the top margin of the window, you can see the buttons with which you can either display the table (*Open*) or switch to Design View. Begin with *Open*.

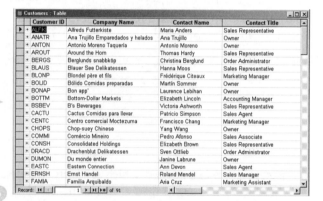

3 The table opens, and the data records are visible. To the left you can see which data record is currently displayed and how many records the table currently contains. Close the table by clicking on the *Close* button.

4 Now switch to the Design mode by clicking on the corresponding button.

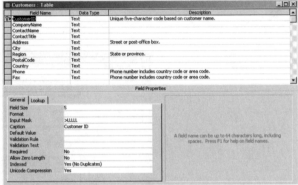

5 Examine the table structure. Each column contains one field, which contains a field name, a field data type, and a field description.

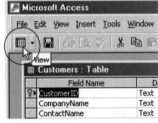

6 To the left on the Toolbar you will find a symbol which allows you to switch directly from one view to the other (toggle between views). It always shows the currently inactive mode, hence Data Sheet View, ...

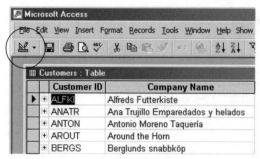

7 ... and after clicking on the button again, the Design View is reinstated.

8 When you click on the small black triangle next to the symbol, the various views are displayed.

A brief checklist

In this chapter, you have learnt a few database basics and gained insights into a professionally designed Access 2000 database. Do you still remember all the terminology? This brief gap-filling exercise will help you memorise the most important terms from the database world .

The DBMS acronym stands for _____ (1). It refers to the software with which a database is managed.

Databases consist of _____ (2), forms, _____ (3), reports, macros, and modules.

The core of a database is formed by tables, linked to each other. A database with links is called _____ (4).

In a table every column is referred to as _____ (5) The column heading is also the field name. To pre-define the column heading or contents its _____ (6) has to be modified.

Access 2000 can be started either with the _____ (7) or with the shortcut bar.

An Access 2000 database is saved in a file with the _____ (8) extension.
The file may have a size of up to _____ (9).

The default database folder is defined with the menu command _____ (10).

The tables in the *Northwind.mdb* example database are linked. The links can be viewed with the _____ (11) menu command.

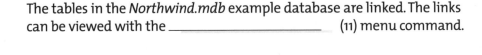

The Database window contains _____ (12)
modules. With the _____ (13) button an object
(for example, a table) can be viewed in Design View. On the left in the
toolbar you can find a symbol with which you can immediately switch
the table into _____ (14).

Answers to this checklist can be found in the Appendix.

What's in this chapter:

In this workshop you are going to work with
the most important element of a database: the
table. After having worked through this chapter,
you will know what a table structure is, and the
terms table field and data record will be
familiar to you. Of course, you are also going
to learn how to enter data, scroll through
tables, and sort by individual fields.
This should enable you
to design all kinds of
new tables and to
record data.

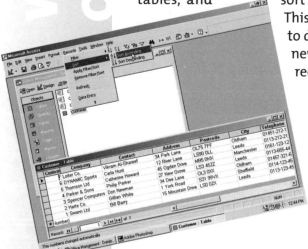

You already know about:

You are going to learn about:

In this workshop you are going to create a new database which consists of several tables. As you already know from the chapter on database basics, tables form the basis of everything the Access program has to offer. Therefore, when you are planning a database, you must first consider which tables it is going to contain.

Take for example an **Office Management System**. As an administrator or a secretary, you constantly deal with a lot of different types of data. If you use Access privately the amount of data is not as large, but you will notice that even a private database may contain several tables. Why don't you try to draw up a list of possible tables for your database?

Customers

In the office this table is an absolute must. Use it for letters, labels, phone numbers, and address lists, and for the analysis of contacts, turnover, orders, and so on. Apart from complete address details with phone number and e-mail, your company contact person must be included. Often there is also a field with remarks on the contact person (hobbies, likes and dislikes for possible presents).

Products

Products which are sold by the company, regular products, stock, individual prices, purchase and sales prices. Do not forget parameters (litres, kg, and packaging) for targeted analyses. The EAN (European Article Number) is often listed as a key field.

Private collections

Your CD collection with title, artist, category, number of pieces, and assessment criteria; a recipe database, an electronic wine cellar, and so on.

Lessons and training

Teachers create student records, and, related to these, lesson or tutorial contents and contact periods. They can then connect the whole into a lessons management system. Sports coaches use Access to plan tournaments, matches, and their league.

It is important that you use the database specifically for the purpose for which you have created it. Do not try to carry out tasks that would be better taken care of by another program. If, for example, you only want to plan your appointments, it would be better to use Outlook. Excel is the more suitable tool if you need to calculate your tax return. Access is most of all suitable for recording, maintaining, managing, and analysing large amounts of data.

New tables

Your first table is going to contain your business partners' and customers' addresses. Companies store customer records up to any size. Even private users can benefit from an address index, provided it is properly maintained.

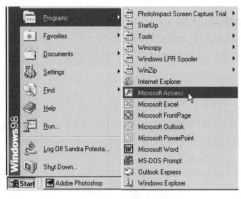

1 Start Access 2000 with the Start menu.

2 Choose the first *Blank Access database* option to create a new database.

3 Confirm the option with *OK*.

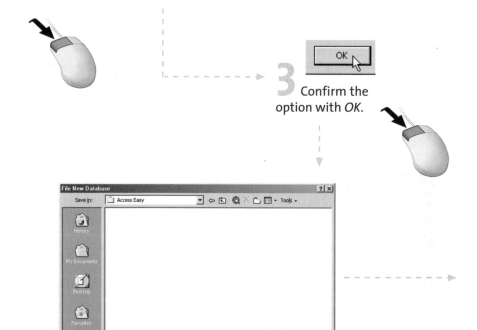

4 As this database will not only contain address data, we should call it *Office Management*. Enter the file name without the extension, ...

5 ... and confirm with
the *Create* button.

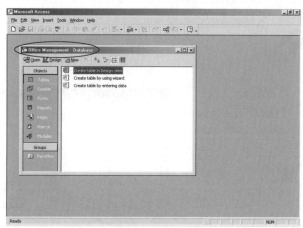

6 The database is created and immediately saved. In the
Title bar, you can see the database name.

7 In the left-hand margin, you can see a Toolbar
with the *Objects* title. The *Tables* object is currently
active, but is empty. Click on other objects and then
return to *Tables*.

Create table in Design view
Create table by using wizard
Create table by entering data

8 In the Tables window you can see three Wizards. Start the first one, which helps you create a new table, by double-clicking on it.

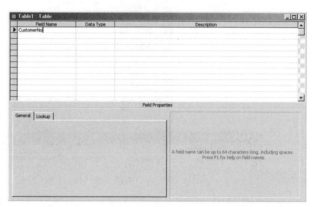

9 Now you can see the design window of the table. Write the first field name 'CustomerNo' (without spaces!).

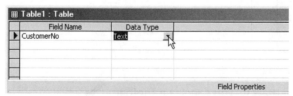

10 Press the ⏎ key to get to the next column. Open the list containing the field data types.

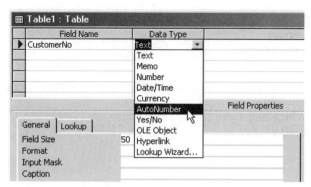

11 The customer number should increment automatically. This is what the *AutoNumber* field data type is for.

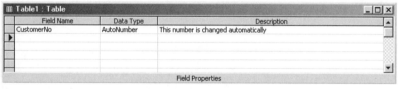

12 Press the ⏎ key to go to the next column, and enter the name for this field. By pressing the ⏎ key you will go to the next row.

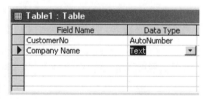

13 Now create the first text field for the company name. Confirm the field data type by pressing the ⏎ key.

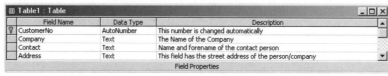

Field Name	Data Type	Description	
CustomerNo	AutoNumber	This number is changed automatically	
Company	Text	The Name of the Company	
Contact	Text	Name and forename of the contact person	
▶			
		Field Properties	

14 After the description, insert a field for your company contact. The more fields you create, the easier it is to analyse the data later on.

Field Name	Data Type	Description	
⚷ CustomerNo	AutoNumber	This number is changed automatically	
Company	Text	The Name of the Company	
Contact	Text	Name and forename of the contact person	
Address	Text	This field has the street address of the person/company	
		Field Properties	

15 Another text field is reserved for the address, ...

Field Name	Data Type	Description	
⚷ CustomerNo	AutoNumber	This number is changed automatically	
Company	Text	The Name of the Company	
Contact	Text	Name and forename of the contact person	
Address	Text	This field has the street address of the person/company	
Postcode	Text	This is the Postcode of the person/company	
		Field Properties	

16 ... and the postcode field also uses this field data type.

Field Name	Data Type	Description
CustomerNo	AutoNumber	This number is changed automatically
Company	Text	The Name of the Company
Contact	Text	Name and forename of the contact person
Address	Text	This field has the street address of the person/contact
Postcode	Text	This is the postcode of the person/company
City	Text	This is the City
Telephone Number	Text	The telephone number of the person/company
Fax Number	Text	The fax number of the person/company

Field Properties

17 You still have to enter the city (text field) and the customer phone numbers. Designate one field each for the phone and the fax numbers.

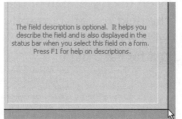

The field description is optional. It helps you describe the field and is also displayed in the status bar when you select this field on a form. Press F1 for help on descriptions.

18 If the field list is too small, you can enlarge the box by dragging it to make it bigger. Grasp it at the bottom right-hand corner; hold down the mouse button and drag.

Field Name	Data Type	Description
CustomerNo	AutoNumber	This number is changed automatically
Company	Text	The Name of the Company
Contact	Text	Name and forename of the contact person
Address	Text	This field has the street address of the person/contact
Postcode	Text	This is the postcode of the person/company
City	Text	This is the City
Telephone Number	Text	The telephone number of the person/company
Fax Number	Text	The fax number of the person/company

Field Properties

19 For now the new table field list is complete. Check again that you have entered all the field names correctly.

Field names must comply with the following rules:

Allowed	Not allowed
Maximum of 64 letters and numbers. The name should begin with a letter. Special characters such as spaces, dashes, dollar signs ($) are allowed but should be avoided.	Full stop (.), exclamation mark (!), accents (ˆˊ), and square brackets ([]).

Always keep an eye on the lower half of the design window. It displays the properties of the field you are currently editing. For example, the field size of text fields is always 50 (characters). Of course, this is a value you can adjust for each field.

Saving table designs

The Table design for the first table has now been completed. You can save the table now. In the course of this operation, you will come across a new term: the primary key.

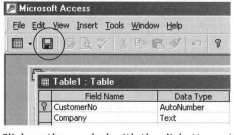

1 Click on the symbol with the diskette on the left in the toolbar.

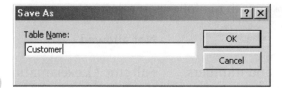

2 Enter the name of the new table.

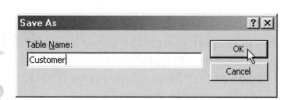

3 Confirm by clicking on the *OK* button to save the table.

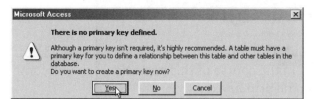

4 Now Access 2000 displays this message box (if the Office Assistant is active, you will see the message in a speech balloon). It reminds you of the primary key. Confirm with *Yes*.

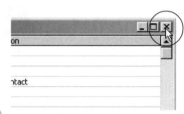

5 The primary key is added to the first field in the table. You can recognise this by the symbol on its left.

6 The table has been saved. You can now close the Design window.

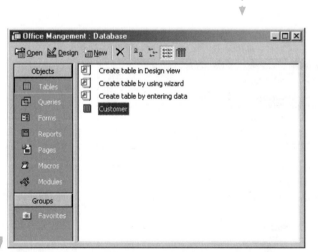

7 This is what your Database window now looks like. In the Table object you can view your first *Customers* table. Clicking on the *Design* button immediately takes you to this table's field list.

What is a **primary key?** Access marks the field in the table that is distinct with the primary key. In this case this is the customer number, which is arrived at with an *AutoValue* field (there are no two identical customer numbers). Access needs the primary key to be able to link tables. There are several types of primary keys, but the distinct primary key is the most common type.

Entering data into tables

Your first table is now ready; you can start entering data. You have already come across the mode you are going to use in the chapter about basic database knowledge: the Data Sheet View is activated to show the data in the table, and to enter, modify, and delete data field by field. The Design View is the mode in which the structure of the table with field names, field data types, and descriptions has been defined.

Let's start entering the customer data. You can always activate the tables in the Table module via the *Open* button. However, it is quicker to double-click on them.

1 The Database window is displayed. In the Group window, you can see that the Table object is active.

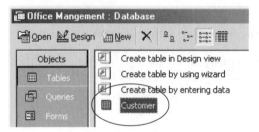

2 Open the table by double-clicking on the symbol or the table name.

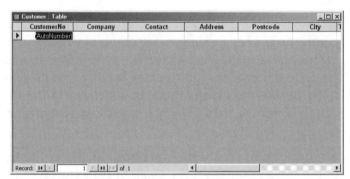

3 The table is ready for data entry; the cursor is flashing in the first field of the first data record.

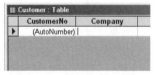

4 You cannot label the first field; it contains the automatically incremented customer number. Press the ⏎ key to switch to the next field.

Customer : Table		
CustomerNo	**Company**	**Cont**
1	Swann Ltd	
(AutoNumber)		

5 Enter the first company name, and press the ⏎ key.

Customer : Table			
CustomerNo	**Company**	**Contac**	**Ad**
1	Swann Ltd		
(AutoNumber)			

6 The field for the company contact is too small. Point to the right-hand column border, ...

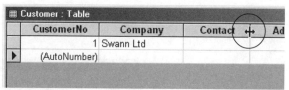

Customer : Table			
CustomerNo	**Company**	**Contact**	**Addre**
1	Swann Ltd		
(AutoNumber)			

7 ... and enlarge the column by simply dragging to the right.

57

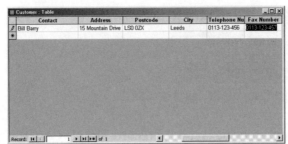

8 Complete the first data record. When you press the ⏎ key, the cursor jumps to the next field.

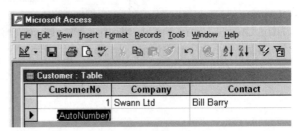

9 Confirm the entry in the last field with the ⏎ key. The cursor jumps to the first field in the second data record. You can start entering the next customer's details.

And these are the remaining customers, which you are now going to add to your customer table:

Cust. No	Company	Contact	Street	Postcode	City	Phone	Fax
1	Swann Ltd	Bill Barry	15 Mountain Drive	LS0 0ZX	Leeds	0113-123-456	0113-123-457
2	Harte Co.	Gillian White	1 York Road	S31 99V	Sheffield	0114-123-456	0114-123-457
3	Spencer Computers	Don Newman	34 Dee Lane	OL3 0XX	Oldham	01457-321-654	01457-321-653
4	Parker & Sons	Philip Parker	27 New Grove	LS3 45Z	Leeds	0113-655-441	0113-655-440
5	Thomson Ltd	Catherine Howard	45 Ogden Drive	M95 0Kk	Manchester	0161-123-123	0161-123-122
6	DYNAMIC Sports	Carla Hunt	12 River Lane	LS90 0LL	Leeds	0113-212-211	0113-212-212
7	Loiter Co.	Vikram Al-Shareef	34 Park Lane	OL75 7FF	Oldham	01457-212-112	01457-212-111

TIP

To change the contents of a field, highlight it and press the F2 function key. Now you can move the cursor to the appropriate place in the text with the arrow keys.

As soon as you have entered the last data record, simply close the table by clicking on the cross in the top right-hand corner of the window, or choosing the FILE/CLOSE menu option.

The question asking whether you want to save the changes refers to the layout modifications (column width). Data records, which have been entered into the table, are immediately saved into the active database. As soon as the cursor disappears from the row, Access writes the new customer into the database. This increases data recording safety and, most important, also allows several users to work with the database.

TIP

Keep an eye on the data record marker on the left-hand edge of the row you are currently editing: when it has the shape of a pencil, it means that the data record is being edited. When it has the shape of a black triangle, the whole row has been saved into the database.

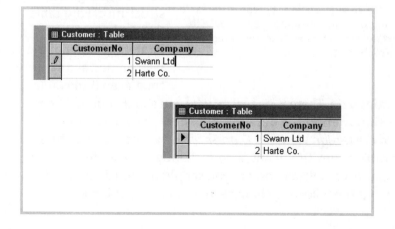

Navigating in the table

In time the table will fill up with more and more data records, and soon the records will not fit onto the screen any more. If you want to

find a particular record or simply scroll through all the records, it is best to use the data record navigator.

The navigator consists of the arrow buttons at the bottom left of the table.

I◀	Click on this symbol to jump to the first data record in the table.
▶I	With this symbol, you can switch to the last data record in the table.
▶	With this arrow, you move the highlight to the next data record.
◀	Clicking on this arrow highlights the previous data record.
1	If you want to go to a particular data record, simply enter its number here.

Changing the table structure

You should never change a field **data type**, if the table already contains data. If, for example, you choose to change a Text field to a Number field, the saved data would definitely be lost.

You can change the structure of your table, that is, the number, name, and order of the field names, at any time, even if the table already contains data. There is no reason why you should not add new fields. Then simply enter the data in Data Sheet View. The strict separation of the *Design View* and *Data Sheet View* modes makes these changes possible at any time. ('Any time' is slightly exaggerated. As soon as the table has been linked to others, you should not touch its structure again.) Carry out the following changes in your customer table:

➡ Reduce the field size of the text fields 'Company', 'Name', and 'First Name' to 30 digits. That should be more than enough.

➡ Add two more fields for *e-mail* and *Internet*. *E-mail* is a Text field in which addresses for electronic mail are going to be entered. *Internet* is going to contain Web page addresses of your customers' homepages, provided they have one. Assign the *Hyperlink* field type to this field.

➡ A further new field is designated to record the marital status of your customer. However, you are going to list possible answers (single, married, and so on) in a drop-down list.

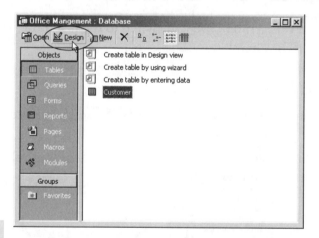

1 Mark the table in the *Tables* object of the database window, and open it in *Design View*.

61

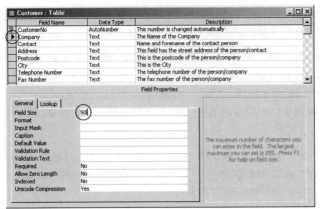

Field Name	Data Type	Description
CustomerNo	AutoNumber	This number is changed automatically
Company	Text	The Name of the Company
Contact	Text	Name and forename of the contact person
Address	Text	This field has the street address of the person/contact
Postcode	Text	This is the postcode of the person/company
City	Text	This is the City
Telephone Number	Text	The telephone number of the person/company
Fax Number	Text	The fax number of the person/company

Field Properties

General | Lookup

Field Size	50
Format	
Input Mask	
Caption	
Default Value	
Validation Rule	
Validation Text	
Required	No
Allow Zero Length	No
Indexed	No
Unicode Compression	Yes

The maximum number of characters you can enter in the field. The largest maximum you can set is 255. Press F1 for help on field size.

2 Mark the field *Company*. Place the highlight in the field properties area, ...

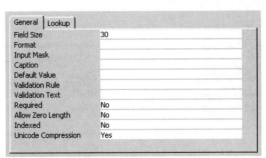

General | Lookup

Field Size	30
Format	
Input Mask	
Caption	
Default Value	
Validation Rule	
Validation Text	
Required	No
Allow Zero Length	No
Indexed	No
Unicode Compression	Yes

3 ... and change the field size. Enter the number 30, and press the ⏎ key. Save the design by clicking on the diskette symbol. A message informs you that with the new field size, data could be deleted. Confirm with *Yes*.

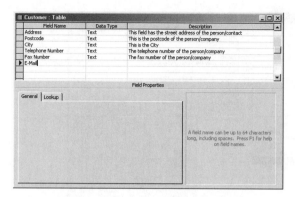

4 Place the cursor in the first field of the next free row, and enter a new field name.

Field Name	Data Type	Description	
Address	Text	This field has the street address of the person/contact	
Postcode	Text	This is the postcode of the person/company	
City	Text	This is the City	
Telephone Number	Text	The telephone number of the person/company	
Fax Number	Text	The fax number of the person/company	
E-Mail	Text	The E-mail Address of the company	

5 Confirm the *Text* field data type and enter the description into the last field in the row.

6 Name the next field *Internet* and apply the *Hyperlink* field data type. Enter a description of the field.

63

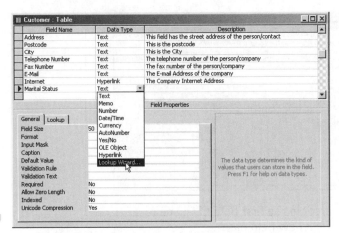

Enter the *Marital Status* field name in the next row.
Use the *Lookup Wizard* for this field.

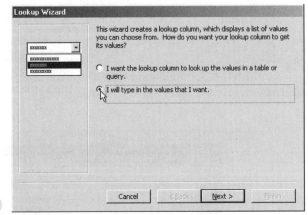

The Wizard starts. Choose the second option, as you do not have a table containing the list contents. Click on *Next* to proceed to the next step.

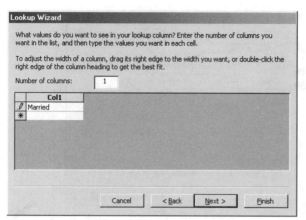

9 As suggested, the list consists of only one column. Enter the first choice to be offered to the user in this field.

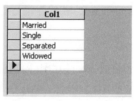

10 Go to the next row by pressing the ⮐ key, and enter the next list entry. Enter all alternatives in the same way.

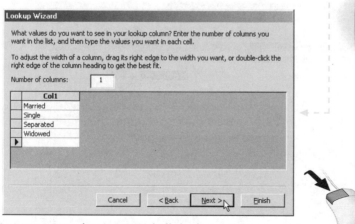

11 As soon as you have entered all the list entries, confirm them by clicking on the *Next* button.

65

12 Now you can assign a name to the field. This name will also be used as the column heading. Click on *Finish*, to complete the field definition.

By clicking on the diskette symbol, you can save your Table design again. With the *View* symbol on the left of the Toolbar, you can immediately switch to the Data Sheet View to enter data for individual customers. When you place your cursor in the *Marital Status* field you will notice that a small arrow appears next to it. Clicking on the arrow opens the drop-down list which you have created with the *Drop-Down List Wizard*.

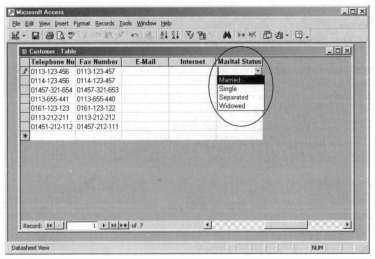

Of course, you can also write in the text yourself, but drop-down lists have the advantage that the contents are standardised in each field. If you wrote 'm' for one customer and 'married' for the next, you would have to take that into consideration when running a query to list all married customers.

The new *Hyperlink* field type is also interesting: when you type an entry into the *Internet* field, it is automatically turned into a hyper-link. A hyperlink is a link to an Internet page or to another document in one of the Office applications. When you place the mouse pointer on one of these hyperlinks (always blue and underlined), it turns into a pointing hand. A single click then opens the Web page or the Office document (a Word text, an Excel spreadsheet, and so on). Of course, you have to be equipped for Internet access, that is, you have to have a modem or an ISDN card and have a current Internet account.

A list of field data types that you can use in a table design is provided below:

Data type	Description	Maximum size
Text	All kinds of text entries and numbers which are not used for calculations	255 bytes
Memo	Longer texts, descriptions, annotations about data records	65,535 bytes
Number	Numbers and values	Depending on the field size 1 byte to 8 bytes
Date	Date and time values. The date calculation starts in the year 100 and ends in 9999.	8 bytes
Currency	Currency values with up to four decimals	8 bytes
AutoValue	Automatically incrementing numbers	4 bytes

Data type	Description	Maximum size
Yes/No	Only accepts the *Yes* or *No* value.	1 bit
OLE object	Images and objects from other applications	1 gigabyte
Hyperlink	Text which can be used as hyperlink addresses	2,048 characters per address part
Drop-Down List Wizard	Creates a drop-down list with entered values or values from other tables	Field size of the other table

Changing the table layout

The table layout is the way the table looks, and of course this does not need to stay the same. You can reduce or enlarge columns, as you saw when you were entering your first data, hide or show columns, and – if you want to – enter different column headings. Let's change the Customer table layout:

⊞ Customer : Table		
CustomerNo ↔	**Company**	**Con**
▶ 1	Swann Ltd	Bill Barry
2	Harte Co.	Gillian White
3	Spencer Computers	Don Newman
4	Parker & Sons	Philip Parker
5	Thomson Ltd	Catherine Hov

Point to the dividing line between the first and the second column of the table.

⊞ Customer : Table		
Custom	**Company**	**C**
▶	1 Swann Ltd	Bill Barry
	2 Harte Co.	Gillian Whit
	3 Spencer Computers	Don Newma
	4 Parker & Sons	Philip Parke
	5 Thomson Ltd	Catherine H

2 Holding down the left mouse button, drag the column to the left. The column is reduced as soon as you release the mouse button.

⊞ Customer : Table				
Custom	**Company**	**Contact**	**Address**	**P**
▶	1 Swann Ltd	Bill Barry	15 Mountain Drive	LS0 0
	2 Harte Co.	Gillian White	1 York Road	S31 9
	3 Spencer Computers	Don Newman	34 Dee Lane	OL3 C
	4 Parker & Sons	Philip Parker	27 New Grove	LS3 4
	5 Thomson Ltd	Catherine Howard	45 Ogden Drive	M95 C
	6 DYNAMIC Sports	Carla Hunt	12 River Lane	LS90
	7 Loiter Co.	Vikram Al-Shareef	34 Park Lane	OL75
*	(Number)			

3 Mark the *Company Contacts* column by clicking on the column heading.

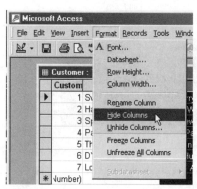

4 From the FORMAT menu, select the HIDE COLUMNS entry. The column disappears from the table.

69

Format Records Tools Win

A Font...
    Datasheet...
    Row Height...
    Column Width...

    Rename Column
    Hide Columns
    Unhide Columns...
    Freeze Columns
    Unfreeze All Columns

    Subdatasheet

5 With the FORMAT/UNHIDE
COLUMNS menu command you
can activate the column again.

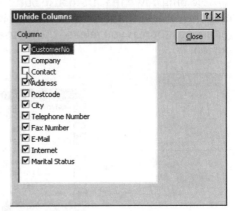

Unhide Columns   ? X

Column: Close

☑ CustomerNo
☑ Company
☐ Contact
☑ Address
☑ Postcode
☑ City
☑ Telephone Number
☑ Fax Number
☑ E-Mail
☑ Internet
☑ Marital Status

6 Tick the column you want to show, and
confirm with *OK*.

Custom	Company	Contact	Address	Postcode	City	Telephone
1	Swann Ltd	Bill Barry	15 Mountain Drive	LS0 0ZX	Leeds	0113-123-45
2	Harte Co.	Gillian White	1 York Road	S31 99VX	Sheffield	0114-123-45
3	Spencer Computers	Don Newman	34 Dee Lane	OL3 0XX	Oldham	01457-321-6
4	Parker & Sons	Philip Parker	27 New Grove	LS3 45ZZ	Leeds	0113-655-44
5	Thomson Ltd	Catherine Howard	45 Ogden Drive	M95 0KK	Manchester	0161-123-12
6	DYNAMIC Sports	Carla Hunt	12 River Lane	LS90 0LL	Leeds	0113-212-2
7	Loiter Co.	Vikram Al-Shareef	34 Park Lane	OL75 7FF	Oldham	01451-212-
(Number)						

7 To hide several columns, you need to select
them with the column headings. Holding down
the mouse button, simply drag the mouse
across the field names.

Tip: You can automatically adjust the COLUMN WIDTH by double-clicking on the line between the columns (in the column heading). The column has now exactly the width required to accommodate the longest column entry.

When you now close the table with the new layout by clicking on the *Close* symbol in the top right-hand corner or by choosing the FILE/CLOSE menu command, the following message is displayed:

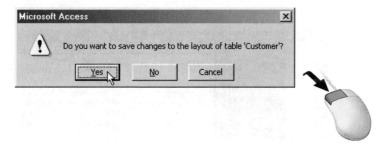

The changes have to be saved, because they have been made in the design of the object table and not in the database data records.

Sorting data

The table is of course not the only display option for your data, but it can be processed with many program functions and moulded into almost any shape. For example, you can sort your customer data by one of the fields, let's say by company names or cities, and then print out the sorted table. Access offers you the possibility of sorting data records alphabetically (ascending or descending). Furthermore, if you wish, you can sort the table by a combination of several columns.

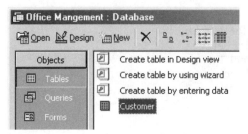

1 In the database window, activate the table by
double-clicking on the table name.

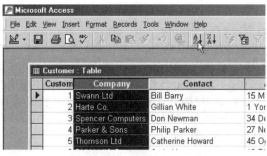

2 To sort the table by company names, place the cursor in
the column with the company names, ...

3 ... and in the Toolbar click on the symbol to sort in
ascending order.

4 Clicking on the symbol with the downward pointing arrow sorts the data records in descending order. Again the criterion is the field in which the cursor is flashing.

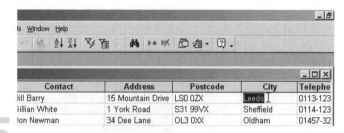

Contact	Address	Postcode	City	Telepho
Bill Barry	15 Mountain Drive	LS0 0ZX	Leeds	0113-123
Gillian White	1 York Road	S31 99VX	Sheffield	0114-123
Don Newman	34 Dee Lane	OL3 0XX	Oldham	01457-32

5 Try out another field: sort the table by cities (it is sufficient to select one field).

To **sort across several fields**, select all the columns you want to sort. This does not mean that the first field is sorted first and then the second, but that all data records that have the same entry in the first sort field are sorted by the second field, and so on.

Filtering tables

To prepare a table so that only the customers in a particular region are displayed, or generally to reduce the display to a specific group of records, you can use the filter functions. A filter is always created for a particular table. Then it can be switched on and off as required. You can even save your filter and then select the appropriate filter for the table you are working with.

You can choose from the following filter types:

↪ The 'Filter by Selection' filter. You simply mark one data record that is similar to the ones you want to extract.

↪ The 'Filter by Form' filter. You enter filter criteria for the whole table into a separate filter window.

↪ The 'Advanced Filter'. Enter the filter criteria into a query window using logical symbols such as =, >, <.

The 'Filter by Selection' filter is used to prepare the table so that it only displays all the Leeds customers, for example.

Address	Postcode	City	Telepho
15 Mountain Drive	LS0 0ZX	Leeds	0113-123
1 York Road	S31 99VX	Sheffield	0114-123
34 Dee Lane	OL3 0XX	Oldham	01457-32
27 New Grove	LS3 45ZZ	Leeds	0113-655
45 Ogden Drive	M95 0KK	Manchester	0161-123
12 River Lane	LS90 0LL	Leeds	0113-212
34 Park Lane	OL75 7FF	Oldham	01451-21

1 In the 'City' field mark the record of a customer from Leeds.

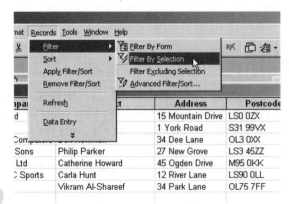

2 Choose the RECORDS/FILTER/FILTER BY SELECTION menu command.

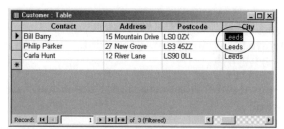

3 The table has been filtered and now you can only see customers from Leeds.

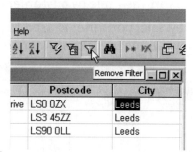

4 In the Toolbar, you can now see that the button with the funnel is engaged. ScreenTips informs you about the symbol.

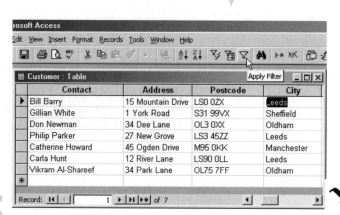

5 When you click on the symbol again, the 'Filter by Selection' filter is removed. The entire table is shown.

The second type of filter is not significantly more complicated. You only have to enter the criterion into a field in the table. Use the 'Filter by Form' to sort the table by customers from a particular region:

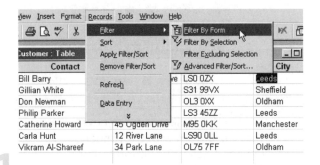

1 Choose the RECORDS/FILTER/FILTER BY FORM menu command.

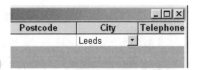

2 The table is reduced to a single row. The filter criterion previously used in the field is suggested. Enter the city 'Oldham'.

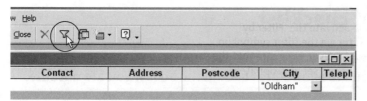

3 Click on the filter symbol, to initiate the filter process by this criterion.

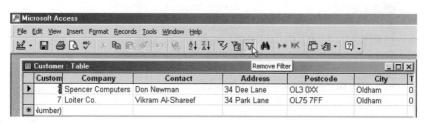

4 The table has been filtered. You can switch off the filter by clicking on the filter symbol.

A brief checklist

In the table below, tick all the statements you think are right. Of course, you are allowed to check in the book if you are not sure.

Statement	Right	Wrong
1. Databases may only contain one table		
2. The MDB file extension marks an Access database		
3. Field names may contain a maximum of 20 letters		
4. There are an infinite number of field data types		
5. The primary key marks a field that appears in all the tables		
6. When entering data in a table, the ⏎ key always switches to the next record		
7. The F2 key opens a highlighted field in which the cursor is flashing		
8. When you can see a pencil on the left-hand edge of a data record, this means that the record has already been saved		
9. In the bottom left-hand corner of the table window, the navigator provides arrows to scroll through the database		

Statement	Right	Wrong
10. You cannot enter numbers in fields that have the *Text* field data type		
11. It is only possible to sort tables in ascending order		
12. The 'Filter by Selection' filter filters the table by the criterion which was displayed before it was activated		
13. Filters remain in the table even after the window has been closed		
14. Phone numbers are numbers and therefore should be stored in fields with the *Number* data type		
15. The *Hyperlinks* field type turns entries into Internet links		

You can find answers to this checklist in the Appendix.

What's in this chapter?

This chapter will introduce you to the
Database Wizard, which takes you step by
step through the creation of a database.
Wizards are indispensable helpers for
designing databases. The example of
Contact Management (addresses) will
illustrate the uses   of   the Wizard, and
outline how you
can employ the
database objects
(tables, forms,
and reports)
created with it.
You will also
learn how
forms can be
edited in the
Form Design,
and how reports are
produced.

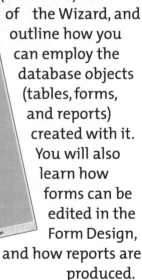

You already know about:

Starting Access 2000	13
Example: the 'Northwind' database	26
New tables	45
Entering data into tables	55
Sorting data	71
Filtering tables	73

You are going to learn about:

Creating new databases with the Wizard	82
Changing the table structure	93
Using forms	100
Changing the form design	104
Editing and producing reports	108

Creating new databases with the Wizard

You will have noticed that careful planning for a database is more difficult than working with the program when you created a new database with a first table, while working through Chapter 2. You need to decide which fields a table should contain; which data types you require; how much data you are going to enter; and so on.

The Database Wizard can take a lot of this workload off your shoulders. With its help, you can create complete table structures. It suggests the most important fields; you only have to choose. Let's have a look at what it offers for address management.

Start Access 2000 by clicking on its symbol in the Start menu.

2 The Start dialog offers the already existing databases. Choose the Database Wizard, ...

3 ... and confirm with *OK*.

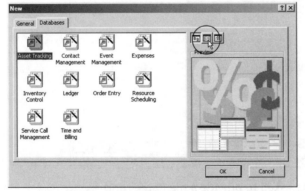

4 A selection of prepared databases appears. The first is already marked. You can see the selection in a different view. Click on the symbol in the middle.

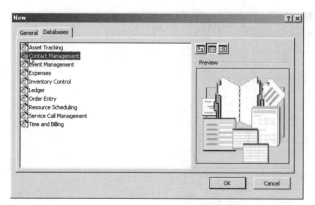

5 This is the List view. Now mark the *Contact Management* database, ...

OK

6 ... and confirm your choice with *OK* to create the database.

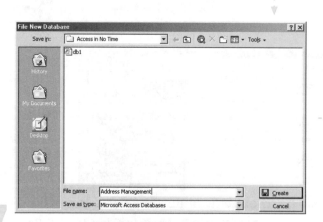

7 Now you are asked to provide a file name for the new database. Enter 'Address Management'.

8 Confirm the new database name.

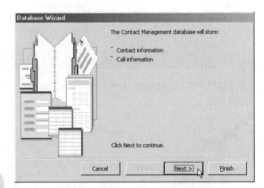

9 Also confirm this message, which informs you about the contents of the new database, and the database can be created.

Now the Wizard will go through the individual fields and make appropriate suggestions. Do you remember? Fields are the table columns. The field name is written above the column. Carefully consider which fields you are going to need. It is better to insert too many than too few fields.

The Wizard suggests the creation of three tables. Under *Contact Information* the addresses will be stored, *Telephone Information* will contain information about telephone contacts, and *Contact Types* will consist of a list with contacts such as *private, business, sports club,* and so on.

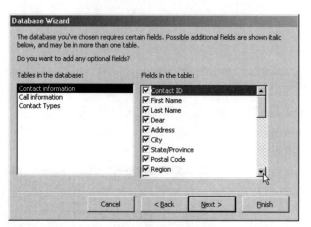

1 The first table has been marked. Scroll through the field list, ...

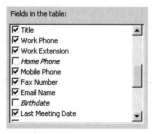

2 ... and have a look at the suggestions in italics, which are not included. You can add fields to the list by ticking them.

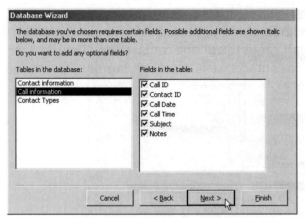

3 Also examine the other two tables, and click on *Next* when you have chosen all the suitable fields.

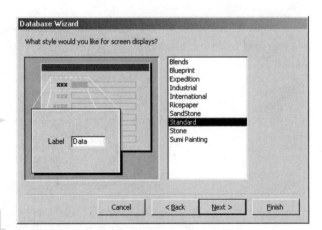

4 Here you can choose a specific style, which includes background, colours, and font. Check the other suggestions such as *International* too, ...

87

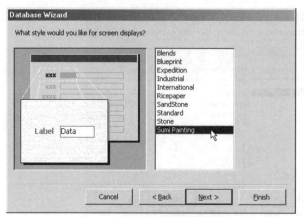

5 ... which includes an image. Every pattern is made attractive in its own way through individual fonts, backgrounds, and colours.

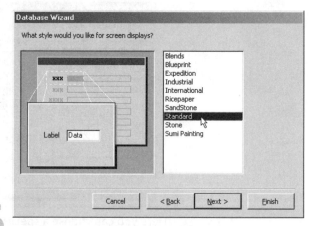

6 Switch to the Standard view. Although it is not very exciting, ...

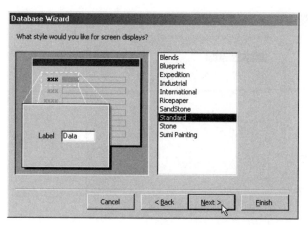

7 ... it is at least easy to edit. Click on the *Next* button to proceed to the next step.

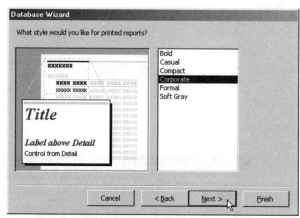

8 You can also apply a style – which provides formatting for headings and for the body text and inserts suitable lines – to reports. Apply the suggested style.

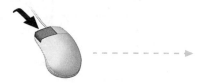

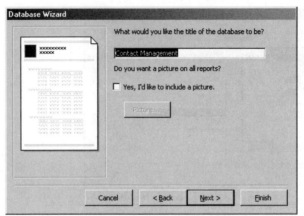

9 Here you can enter the name that is applied to the tables, forms, and reports. The image in the report could, for example, be a company logo (which needs to be available as a file).

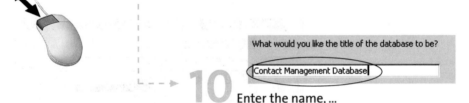

10 Enter the name, ...

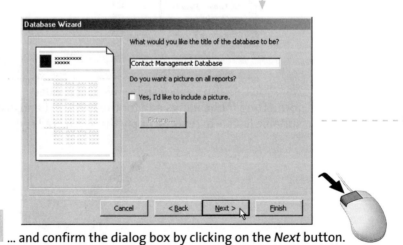

11 ... and confirm the dialog box by clicking on the *Next* button.

12 Complete the work of the Wizard by clicking on the *Finish* button.

13 Now it takes some time for the Wizard to complete creating all the database objects.

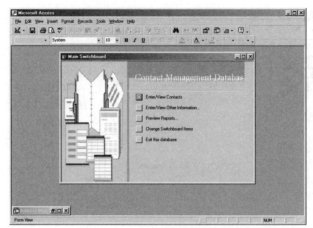

14 Finally, the new database is shown to you in an overview form from which you can simply choose the required database object.

Have a look at the result in the WINDOW menu: the main overview, which is the form which is shown, and the Database window, which has been reduced to a tiny window in the bottom left-hand corner. When you click on the Database window (or choose it from the WINDOW menu), it opens. In it the Form module is active and you can see the forms which are contained in your new database.

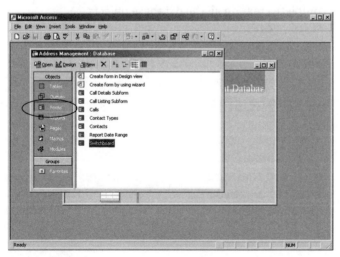

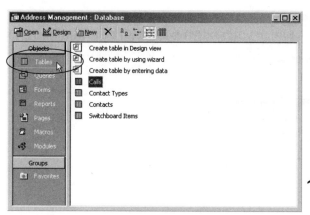

The Table module has four entries. Calls, contact types contacts, and switchboard items (required for the overview form).

The Report module also has something to show. When you switch to the Database window, you will find two reports which have automatically been created by the Wizard.

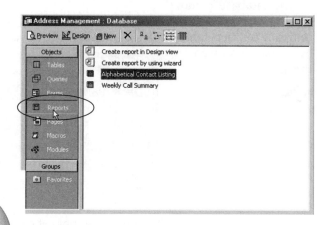

Changing the table structure

Of course, you can adjust the structure of the address table any way you like. You should do this before you start entering data into the table. Examine the fields and their properties, and consider carefully what is useful to you. Delete what you do not need. It is of course also possible to add new fields.

93

What about a validation rule for one of the fields? This ensures that only appropriate data – which you really want – can be entered in this field.

1 The database window is active. Open the company contacts table by double-clicking on the name.

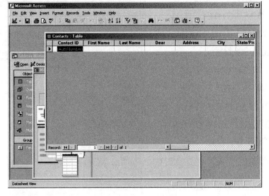

2 The table does not yet contain any data records. With the symbol at the top right you can switch to the structure.

Field Name	Data Type
City	Text
StateOrProvince	Text
PostalCode	Text
Region	Text
Country	Text
CompanyName	Text

3 If you want to delete a row such as the 'Region' field, point to the row and select *design view* at the top left.

4 Press the right mouse button to select the row and open the context menu.

5 Delete the row with the appropriate option.

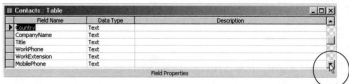

6 The field is removed from the list, and the other fields are moved upwards to fill the gap. Scroll down the list for the next field.

95

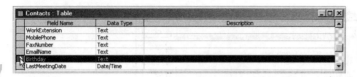

Field Name	Data Type	Description
WorkExtension	Text	
MobilePhone	Text	
FaxNumber	Text	
EmailName	Text	
Birthday	Text	
LastMeetingDate	Date/Time	

7 Select the Birthday field.

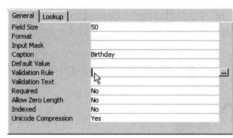

8 In this field, you should not be able to enter any date after the current date. This is called a validation rule. In the field properties, click in the corresponding field.

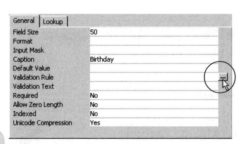

9 Open the formula editor, ...

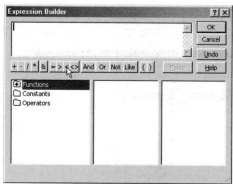

10 ... and enter the operator (less than <).

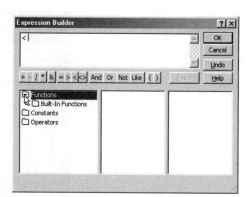

11 Then open the function list by double-clicking on it.

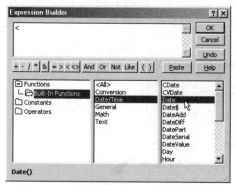

12 Select the Date function in the category of the same name, ...

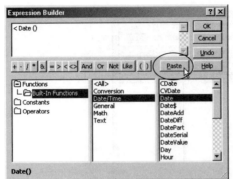

13 ... and paste the function into the formula.
Complete your entries by clicking on the *OK* button.

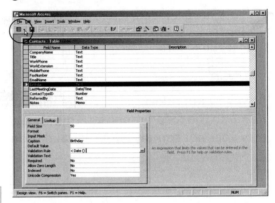

14 The validation rule which restricts the date to
entries which are earlier than the current date is
complete. The formula has been entered. You can now
switch to the data sheet and input data.

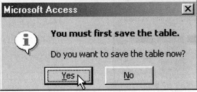

Microsoft Access

ⓘ **You must first save the table.**

Do you want to save the table now?

[Yes]   [No]

15 Just a moment, do not forget to save
the table first.

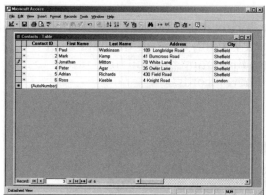

16 Enter a few data records. Move from field to field by pressing the ⏎ key. When you have filled the last field, the record is automatically saved.

The validation rule also includes a validation message, which you enter into the field properties. This message is displayed when an entry does not comply with the validation rule. Another important

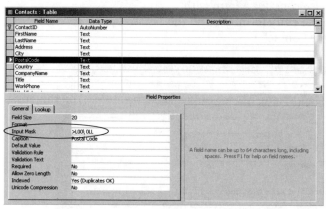

property: the entry format determines the form in which data must be entered. Take a look at the 'Postcode' field format:

The 'Loo\oLL' format ensures that six characters exactly must be entered in the field. The fields for phone numbers are also formatted to ensure a standardised data entry.

99

Using forms

Forms are data entry documents for tables. Each form has a table or a query as its basis. It individually displays the data records contained in the table, and offers the option to scroll from record to record, modify data, and add new records.

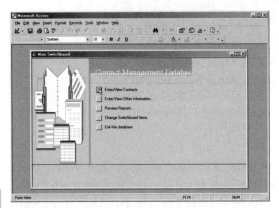

1 The address database contains a form with which you can call up the entry form. Click on the first option (Enter/View Contacts).

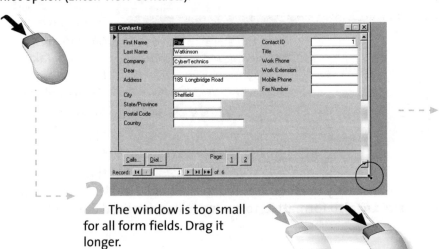

2 The window is too small for all form fields. Drag it longer.

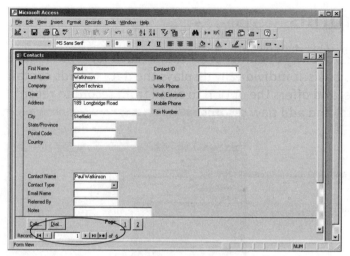

3 Now you can scroll through the data records. Click on the arrows of the data records navigator.

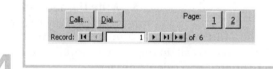

4 You can now scroll through the records one by one, or jump to the start or the end of the table. With the Star symbol you can delete the form for the next new data record.

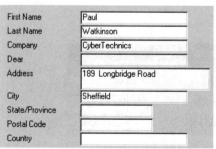

5 You can go to the next field in the form by pressing either the ⬇ or the ⏎ key.

101

6 Enter the next data record.

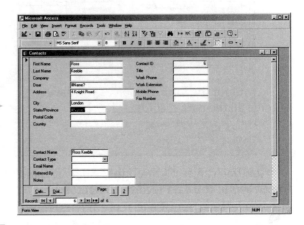

7 Write the address details into the fields, and press the ⏎ key to complete each field.

Record: I◄ ◄ [7] ► ►I ► of 7

8 Whenever you switch to the next or the previous record, the new data record is automatically saved.

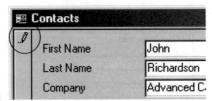

9 Keep an eye on the data record marker. The pencil indicates that the record has not yet been saved.

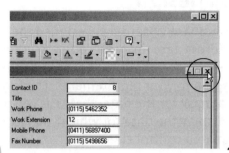

10 Close the form as soon as you have entered all the data records.

The form can also be edited in an alternative view, namely in Data Sheet View. You can switch to this view with the familiar symbol in the top left corner of the screen. The Wizard has also included a button for the Data Sheet View in the form.

Although the Data Sheet View looks like the table, it is nevertheless a form. Enter data the way you enter it into a table. The data record navigator is again placed in the bottom left-hand corner of the window. With the symbol in the top left corner you can switch back to the form. Clicking on the cross in the top right-hand corner closes the window, changing the form design.

A guide to quick scrolling in forms:
With Ctrl+Pg↓ or Pg↑ from record to record
With Ctrl+ Home to the first data record, and Ctrl+End to the last record
The F2 function key opens the selected field, and you can then edit the contents. To save a record earlier, simply press ⇧+↵.

Changing the form design

Control elements are those fields in a form in which the individual columns of the table are displayed record by record.

The Database Wizard has designed the form for address data entry. Of course, you can create such forms yourself or change them according to your requirements. The form is only a mask for the data; that is, it will only ever display the data for which you have designated control elements.

Let's change the form. Delete those control elements you do not need, and change the labels and formatting on the form.

1 Close the form window, so that the overview is displayed again. Double-clicking on the title of the Database window, ...

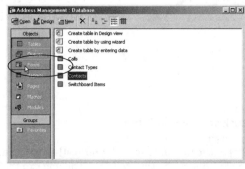

2 ... activates the window. Switch to the Form module.

3 Select the form for the addresses and company contacts, ...

4 ... and open it in Design View.

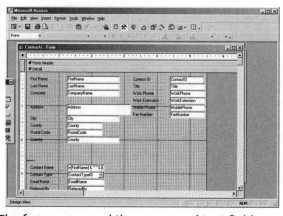

5 The form opens, and the names and text fields are visible in the entry area.

105

Contact ID:	ContactID
Title:	Title
Work Phone:	WorkPhone
Work Extension:	WorkExtension
Mobile Phone:	MobilePhone
Fax Number:	FaxNumber

6 To move a field (including the field name), click on it, and holding down the mouse button, ...

Contact ID:	ContactID
Title:	Title
Work Phone:	WorkPhone
Work Extension:	WorkExtension
Mobile Phone:	MobilePhone
Fax Number:	FaxNumber

7 ... simply drag the two elements downwards.

Contact ID:	ContactID
Title:	Title
Work Phone:	WorkPhone
Work Extension:	WorkExtension
Mobile Phone:	MobilePhone
Fax Number:	FaxNumber

8 To move a whole block of fields, place the mouse pointer above the first field, ...

Contact ID:	ContactID
Title:	Title
Work Phone:	WorkPhone
Work Extension:	WorkExtension
Mobile Phone:	MobilePhone
Fax Number:	FaxNumber

9 ... drag the frame which surrounds each field (it is enough to do it partially), ...

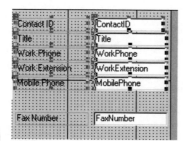

10 ... and release the mouse button.

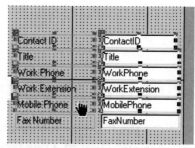

11 Holding down the mouse button, move the selected fields.

12 Now you can save the modified Form Design, ...

107

13... and immediately switch to Form View to edit the data.

Editing and producing reports

Apart from the form for recording and modifying data, the Database Wizard has also created a few reports. Reports are masks for printouts. Data will only be inserted into the respective report fields in the printout. Let's have a look at the reports in the address database.

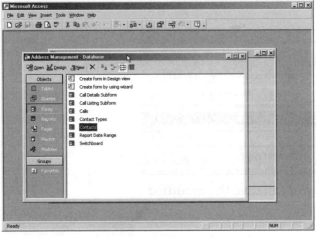

1 Close the form, reactivate the Database window, ...

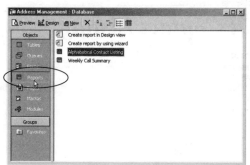

2 ... and switch to the Report module.

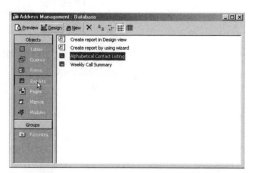

3 Select the first report – an alphabetical list of the recorded address details – and open the Report Design.

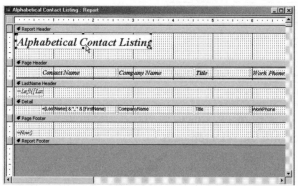

4 Here, too, place the control elements according to your requirements. To enlarge the heading, select it, ...

109

Report Header

Alphabetical Contact Listing

5 ... and move the drag point on the frame to the right.

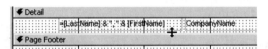

Detail
=[LastName] & "," & [FirstName]   CompanyName

Page Footer

6 To reduce the distance between the addresses, drag the page footer area a little upwards.

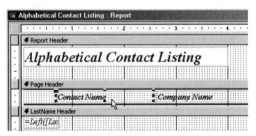

Alphabetical Contact Listing : Report

· · · 1 · · · 1 · · · 2 · · · 1 · · · 3 · · · 1 · · · 4 · ·

Report Header

Alphabetical Contact Listing

Page Header
Contact Name   *Company Name*

LastName Header
=Left([Las

7 The text in blue indicates headings. To modify them, click into the selected field again ...

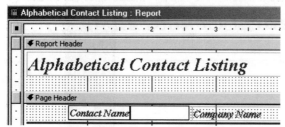

8 ... and change the contents. Delete the text with the Del or the ⬅ key, and enter the new text.

9 Check the finished report in the page preview.

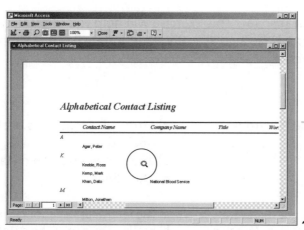

10 The report is displayed page by page on the screen. The mouse pointer turns into a magnifying glass. One click ...

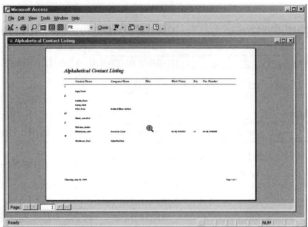

11 ... restores the view to full page size. With the bottom left navigation arrows you can scroll the report. You can print it by clicking on the printer symbol.

The report is automatically filled with data from the table. When you have recorded new addresses, simply produce a new report. Also take a look at the other report in the Report module. Open it in Design View, and change the order of its elements.

A brief checklist

Is everything clear so far? This exercise will help you to recall the most important terms. Have a go at it; it will definitely pay off! Simply tick the right answer.

Question	Answer
1. The Database Wizard is started ...	a) after a database has been opened b) after Access has been started c) after dinner
2. The Wizard suggests several styles for the screen. This refers to ...	a) the length of the data records b) setting the size of the database c) formatting the screen forms with fonts and backgrounds

Question	Answer
3. When the Wizard designs a database it contains ...	a) a database window with tables, forms, and reports b) only forms and no database window c) only data
4. A validation rule for a table field, prescribes ...	a) how quickly a field will be displayed b) what can be entered into the field by the user c) which font is used in the field
5. A form is the entry mask for ...	a) all tables of a database b) a single table (or query) of a database c) a tax return
6. Control elements are ...	a) monthly data for the Inland Revenue b) fields in the Table Design c) fields in the Form Design
7. The report automatically shows ...	a) all data from the table or query it is based on b) a list of all files on the hard disk c) all the control elements of a form
8. The *Date()* formula which can be used in the validation rule ...	a) resets the current date by one day b) contains the current date c) bars the current date from being used
9. The main overview which is produced by the Wizard is ...	a) a program error b) a form c) a report
10. The middle of the three top right boxes in the database window ...	a) maximises the database window b) closes the database window and thus the database c) switches to the *Solitaire* card game

Answers to this brief checklist can be found in the Appendix.

4

What's in this chapter?

In this workshop you are going to use the Wizard again. This time you are going to create a relational database with its help, thus increasing your knowledge of field structure. In Form Design you will get to know additional options for editing control elements. Furthermore, you are going to create and design a form by yourself. How to create a report is also outlined in this chapter.

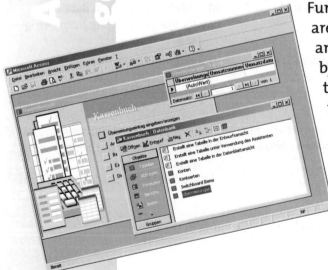

Creating a cashbook

Later you can simply copy together the objects (tables, forms, and reports) from different databases, as MDBs can contain many different objects.

For your new database start the Wizard again, and follow the instructions to the end. The result is a further MDB file with database objects such as tables, forms, and reports.

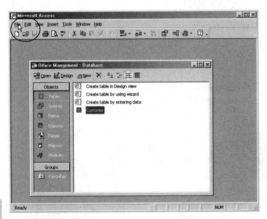

1 If there is an open database, simply activate the FILE menu.

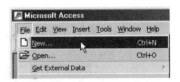

2 Create a new database.

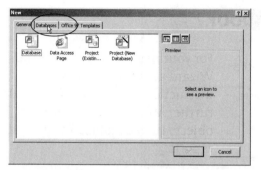

3 The open database has been closed. Switch to the *Databases* tab in which the Wizards are listed.

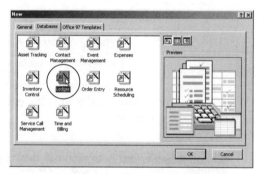

4 Create a cashbook database with this Wizard.

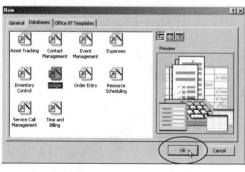

5 Start the Wizard.

6 Access suggests a name for the new database.
Type in a name of your choice.

7 Do not type in the file extension, as Access 2000
automatically adds the extension (MDB for Microsoft
DataBase).

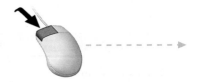

8 Now you can create the new database.

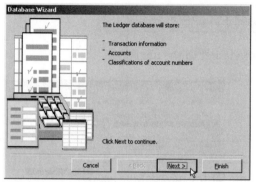

9 The database has been created, and the Wizard starts asking you questions. Click on *Next*.

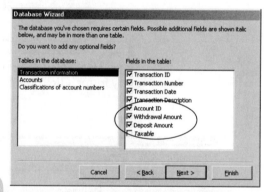

10 Take a look at the field list in the first table. Although you can deselect the fields, they are all required for the Wizard.

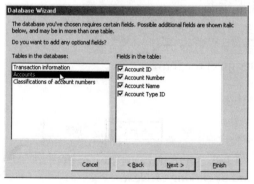

11 Also, check the other tables and their field lists.

12 Press the *Next* button to get to the next step.

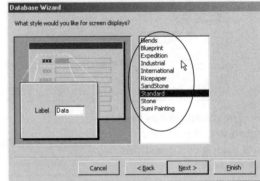

13 Here you define the appearance of the data entry forms. Click on a template, ...

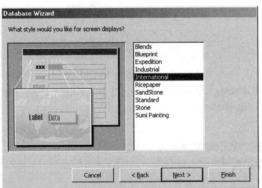

14 ... and check the design of the forms.

15 Proceed to the next step of the Wizard by clicking on *Next*.

120

16 Here you can choose from different report designs. Choose the first template.

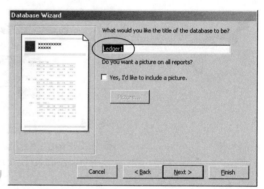

17 In the next step, enter a name for the tables, forms, and reports.

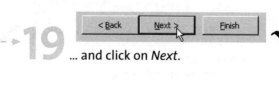

What would you like the title of the database to be?

Cashbook

18 Enter the name of the new database, ...

< Back   Next >   Finish

19 ... and click on *Next*.

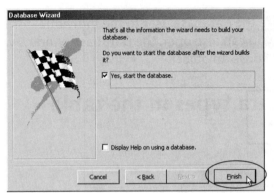

20 Click on *Finish* to set up the new database.

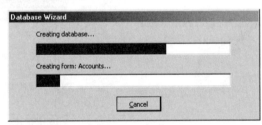

21 You need to exercise some patience. The objects need to be created.

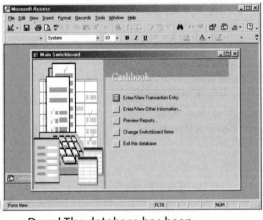

22 Done! The database has been completed! A form with the title 'Main Overview' is provided for the individual objects.

Overview forms take the database user to the individual forms and reports. Of course, you can also open the Database window with the Window menu to choose an object.

New field data types in the table structure

WHAT'S THIS?

Field data types prescribe which contents the fields may have (for example, Number for numerical values, dates, and currencies).

As you already know from previous chapters, the field structure is the basis of everything. The correct choice of field data types guarantees that the database functions optimally. You can find a list of all field data types in the previous chapter. Now you can familiarise yourself with some more field data types and field properties for your tables.

1 Activate the Database window either with the Window menu or by clicking on the symbol in the task list.

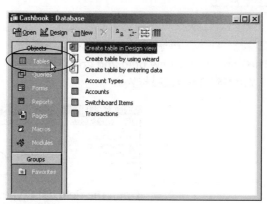

2 Switch to the Table module.

3 You can activate the design by clicking once on the table for the accounts.

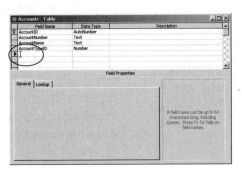

4 To add a new field, click on the first field of an empty row.

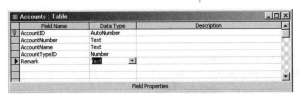

5 Enter the name of the new field and go to the next column by pressing the ⇆ key.

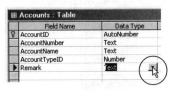

6 Open the field data types list, ...

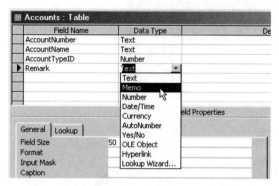

7 ... and choose the *Memo* type.

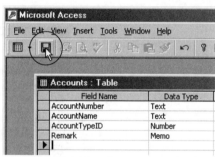

8 The new field has been created. You can save the Table Design again, ...

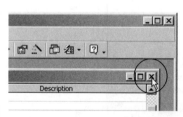

9 ... and then close the window.

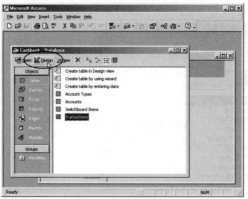

10 Now you are going to change the *Transactions* table. Switch to Design View after selecting the table.

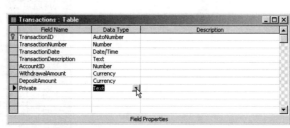

11 Again, enter the new field into the first free field. Specify the *Yes/No* data type.

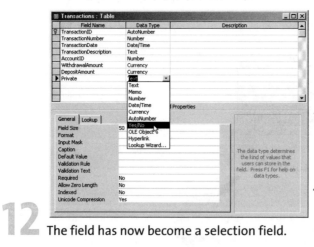

12 The field has now become a selection field.

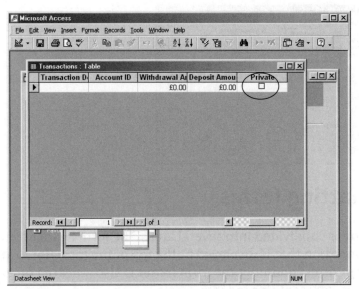

13 You can save the design and immediately switch into Data Sheet View. Here you can see that a check box has been provided in the *Yes/No* field.

Memo fields can contain up to 65,535 characters and are particularly suitable for descriptions, annotations, and so on. The Yes/No field is used if there are only two options.

In the field structure you will have noticed a few fields of the Number data type, which refer to numbers in other tables. The account type number in the Account table, for example, is listed with the 'Long Integer' size. It refers to the Primary Key field in the 'Account types' table.

To arrange the windows in this display more clearly, simply move them: place the mouse pointer on the Title bar and drag the window while holding down the mouse button. You can enlarge and reduce windows by dragging their corners and edges.

You can examine the relationships between individual tables, after choosing the TOOLS/RELATIONSHIPS menu command.

127

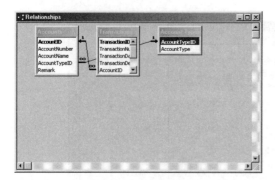

Formatting forms

Each form is subdivided into several areas. The form header contains the information that is displayed at the top of the form (for example, the title). Correspondingly, the form footer is also repeated on each page. It usually contains buttons.

Each form can contain a page header and footer. Information in these areas is displayed on every page of the form. Finally, the Detail area displays the individual data records with their fields.

Let's take a look at our cashbook entry form. We are also going to insert a formatted title into the form header.

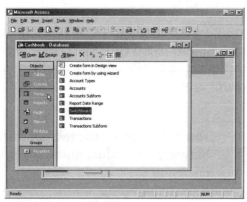

To be able to edit the main form, switch to the Forms module in the Database window, ...

... and open the Account form in Design View.

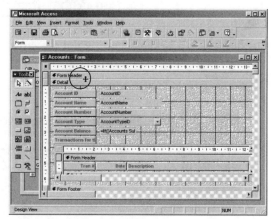

The Form Design is displayed. The *Form Header* area is still empty. Place the mouse pointer on the bottom edge of this area, ...

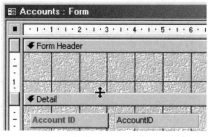

... and drag it downward to enlarge the area.

5 Now you can switch to the *Label* tool in the toolbox.

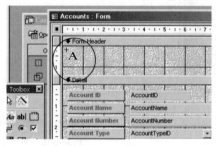

6 Point the crosshairs into the top left-hand corner, ...

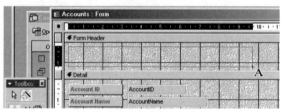

7 ... and, holding down the left mouse button, drag open a rectangle in the form header.

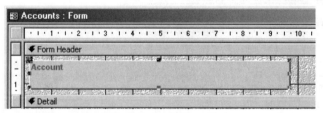

8 The new element has been inserted. You can now enter a title for the form.

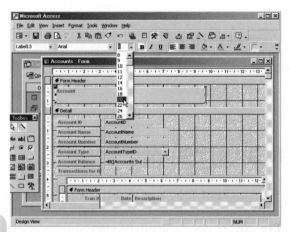

9 When you have finished entering the text, click into the form area and then on the frame of the element. You can then apply a different font size to it.

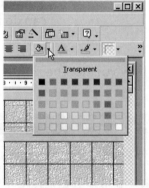

10 In the Toolbar, you can find further symbols for the selected element, such as background colour, font colour, and other formatting.

The **Toolbox** is the toolbox for the Form Design. When you place the mouse pointer on one of the elements, ScreenTips will display what it has to offer.

Now save your form again, and switch to data entry. The form now contains a title. You can also change the formatting of existing form elements. Point to an individual element, click on it, and apply the new formatting by clicking on the appropriate symbol.

Properties of form elements

Every part of the form and the form itself has a list of properties that can be called up in the Properties window. Within this window, you can modify properties such as font size, or you can do it with the Toolbar symbol.

This is how you list the properties on the form:

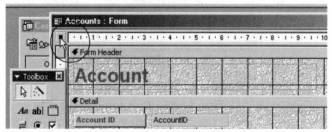

1 First you have to switch back to the form Design View. Point to the box at the top left of the Form window.

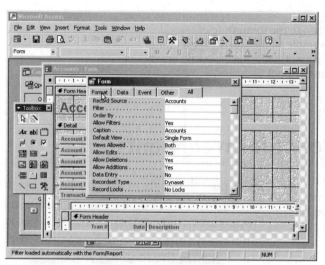

2 Double-clicking opens the Properties window of the form, which contains five tabs.

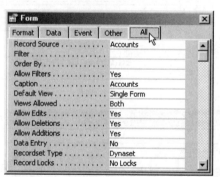

3 All the properties are listed in the *All* tab. The other tabs display subcategories which sum up individual groups.

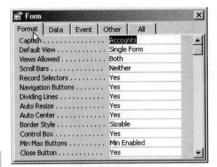

4 The formatting characteristics of the form, such as background, pattern, and scroll bars are located in the *Format* tab.

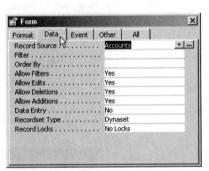

5 *Data* shows which tables can be edited with the form.

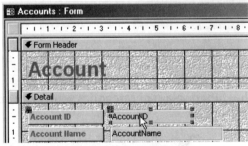

6 Check the properties of one of the elements on the form, for example the account number. Select the element.

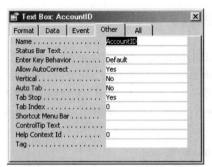

7 The Properties window now shows formatting, contents, and links for this element.

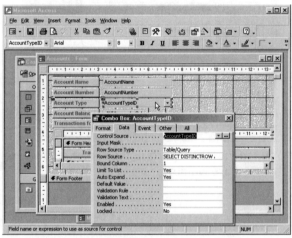

8 For Account Types the Wizard has created a combination field that obtains its numbers from the *Account Types* table with a SELECT instruction in Data Origin.

9 With this symbol, you can switch the Properties window off and on when required. (However, double-clicking on one of the elements also opens the window).

135

Editing report elements

Apart from tables and forms, the Wizard has also created a number of reports, which you can print out or edit. Reports are the means with which the data from the tables are committed to paper. When you examine the Report Wizard, you will notice that there are many possible variations.

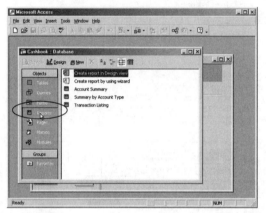

1 You can find the reports in the Report module of the Database window.

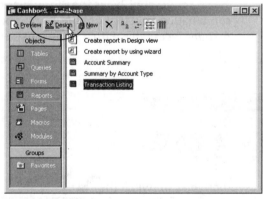

2 Open the 'Transaction List' report in Design View.

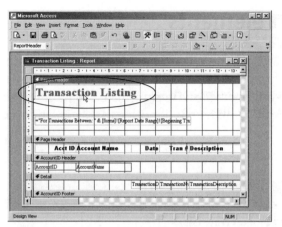

3 You can format these elements in the same way as you have formatted form elements: when you double-click on the element, ...

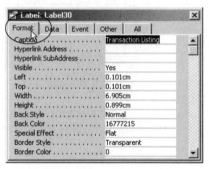

4 ... the Properties window offers you all the contents and formatting so that you can edit them.

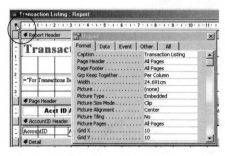

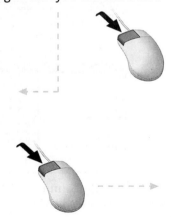

5 Activate the properties of the report.

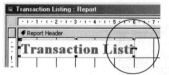

6 If an element is too small or too short, drag it to the appropriate size by means of one of the drag points.

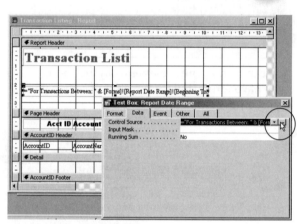

7 Some elements contain formulas to calculate their contents. To display these completely, open the Editor.

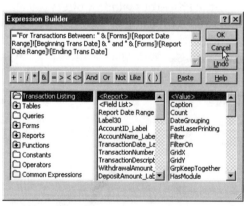

8 Here the formula is listed in its entirety and can also be edited.

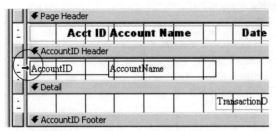

9

The header area contains the field elements, which are filled with data when they are printed out. To format them, select the whole row.

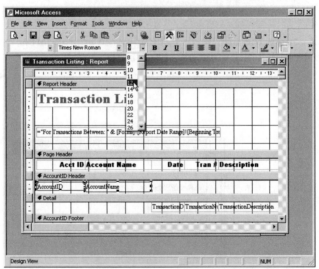

10

Apply a new font size to the selected elements.

11 Of course, the title needs to be adjusted appropriately, here for example with white script on a black background.

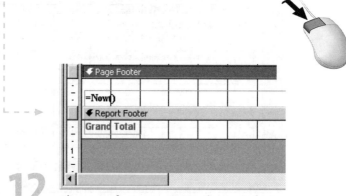

12 The page footer contains the text that appears on every report page in the footer area. The footer area (the report footer) contains what is printed at the end of the report (usually the total).

13 On the right-hand side you can find complex formulas for subtotals, serial numbers, and the total of the report.

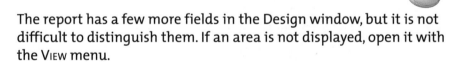

14 Then switch back to print preview to start the report.

The report has a few more fields in the Design window, but it is not difficult to distinguish them. If an area is not displayed, open it with the VIEW menu.

Report header   The contents of this area are printed at the beginning of the report.

Page header   The fields and text elements that are placed here are printed on every page of the report.

Header area   Contains the field name which is planned as a group (with field name). Fields assigned as group fields can be defined with the VIEW/SORT AND GROUP menu command.

Details area	These are the data records, which are listed under the group in the header area. If no grouping has been specified, all data records are printed here.
Page footer	This contains information to be repeated on every page (for example, page numbers).
Report footer	This area contains everything you want to be printed at the end of the report.

After you have become familiar with your new database forms and reports, enter your first data. First you should record the account types, then your accounts, and finally the first transfers.

Check the page numbers in the page footer: you can enter page numbers in this or a similar way in every report. The Wizard uses a text box with the =PAGE() formula. The page number is entered in the Properties window as the contents of the text field's control elements.

A brief checklist

Here is another exercise to back up your knowledge. Have a go at filling in the gaps in this text. If you are unsure about something, feel free to look it up in the book.

To create a new database in the Access 2000 window, open the _____ (1) menu. You can only ever have _____ (2) database open. An open database is automatically closed, when you open or create a new database. The data records are already saved, as they are saved during_____ (3). The Memo field can contain up to_____ (4) characters. As opposed to the text field, this is used for annotations and remarks. The relationships between individual tables can be found under _____ (5) in the_____ (6) menu.
Forms are divided into areas. The title is usually contained in the _____ (7), the data in the_____ (8). If you want to select more than one control element in the form, drag a frame around the elements with the _____ (9). The elements _____ (10) must be completely surrounded by the frame. To call up the properties of an element, _____ (11) on the *Properties* symbol. The _____ (12) property shows with which table the form is linked.
Reports can be found in the _____ (13) of the Database window. Double-clicking on a report opens it in the _____ (14). The mouse pointer turns into a magnifying glass and clicking on the report _____ (15) displays it in Full Page View.
A report is also divided into areas. The heading is contained in the _____ (16), and the data in the_____ (17). Page numbers can always be found in the _____ (18).

What's in this chapter:

Now you are going to create a database without the help of the Wizard. Even though this is more difficult, it will help you to understand individual techniques and connections better. Furthermore, there are Wizards available to you in the individual modules, which will take you safely on to the next step. You will get to know the quickest way to get to forms and reports, and a few tricks which will help you to design databases independently.

You already know about:

You are going to learn about:

A new database

Let's create a new database. To jolt your memory: a database is a file with the MDB extension, which contains tables, queries, forms, reports, and, if required, macros and modules. Data records are automatically saved when they are entered into the database. You need to save all the objects you create for database management.

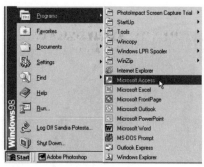

1 Start Access 2000 with the Start menu of your operating system.

2 Create a new database with this option.

3 The name can contain up to 255 letters and numbers. Do not enter the extension, as Access will do that for you.

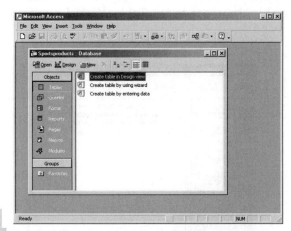

4 The database is complete and has been saved. You can begin to create the first table.

Problems with database names?

Windows is actually very accommodating when it comes to naming files. Nevertheless, file names must comply with a few rules:

When this error message is displayed, you have used a forward slash (/) or backward slash (\) and this is not allowed.

Here the file name contains a character (>) that is not allowed. Only use letters, numbers, spaces, and dashes.

The first table: Products

The first table will contain the products of our sports products database. To ensure that you take into account all the important fields from the beginning, you should leave the task of creating the table structure to the Table Wizard.

Start designing the first table by double-clicking on *Create table by using wizard*.

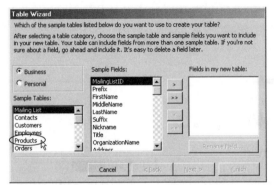

2 The Wizard starts and presents you with a selection of Table Designs. Choose the Products table.

3 The field list adopts the fields of this table. You can adopt all the fields in one go by clicking on the double arrow.

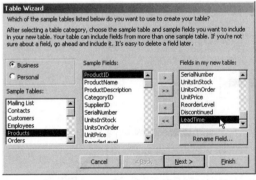

4 Scroll through the list and find the fields you do not need, such as the *Lead Time* field. Select the field name, ...

149

5 ... and send the field back to the list of suggestions.

The Table Wizard offers two categories of tables: the *Business* category contains tables you need for business purposes. Under *Private* you can find a list of suggestions designed for private purposes.

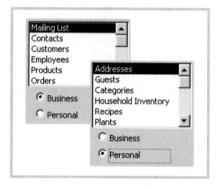

Of course, you do not have to adopt the suggested field names. If you want to rename a field, select it after you have copied it into the right-hand list and click on the *Rename field* button. Enter a name of your choice.

If you find a useful field in one of the other example tables, you can also copy it into your selection list. In Design View you can always add new fields later.

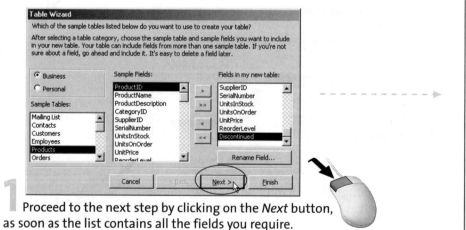

1 Proceed to the next step by clicking on the *Next* button, as soon as the list contains all the fields you require.

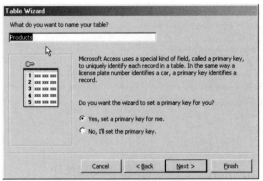

2 Now you need to decide on a name for the table.

What do you want to name your table?

Sports Products

3 Enter it into the entry field above.

Do you want the wizard to set a primary key for you?

● Yes, set a primary key for me.

○ No, I'll set the primary key.

4 The *Yes, set a primary key for me* option ensures that the primary key and a new field at the top of the table are automatically created.

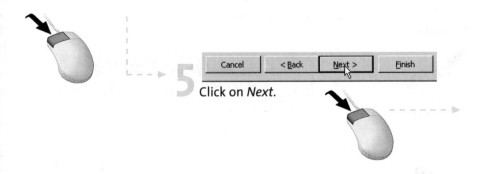

Cancel   < Back   Next >   Finish

5 Click on *Next*.

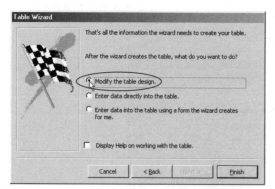

First check the new table in Design View.

Click on *Finish*.

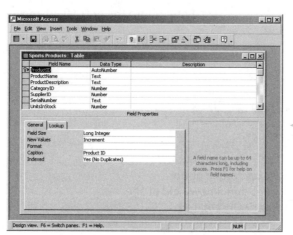

The structure of the new *Sports Products* table is displayed.

Sports Products : Table	
Field Name	Data Type
🔑 ProductID	AutoNumber
ProductName	Text

Keep an eye on the first field, which the Wizard has inserted. It contains the primary key.

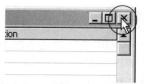

10 Close the Structure window, the table has been saved.

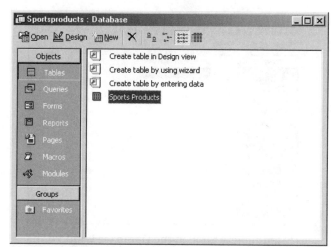

11 The Table module of the Database window now shows the first table.

The Primary Key field is always a field with the *AutoValue* data type. In this way, it is ensured that the field automatically increments with each data record. Whoever inputs the data does not need to enter anything into this field, so errors are absolutely impossible.

WHAT IS THIS?

The **primary key** marks the field which distinguishes the data record, and that is in almost all the cases an ID field at the beginning of the structure (ID = identity). Without a primary key you cannot link the table to other tables.

Check the table structure in the Design window, and add further fields if necessary. The structure of the table should be complete when you start linking the table to other tables.

Table no. 2: Linking categories

In the structure of the *Sports Products* table, there is only a number field reserved for the product category. Therefore you could not record a category such as 'Ski Equipment' in this table. Instead you are going to create a separate table, which contains all the categories, and connect it via a relational link with the first table.

1 Create the new table in the Database window, in the same way as you created the last one.

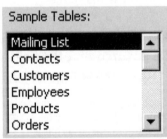

2 Again, the Table Wizard offers its Designs. The *Business* category is selected. Scroll down in the list of example tables.

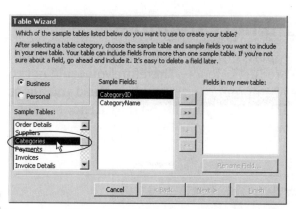

3 Here you will find the appropriate *Categories* table.

4 Copy the two fields into the right-hand list.

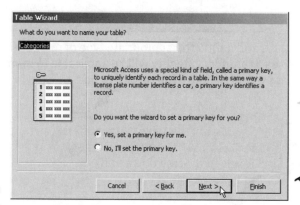

5 You will also adopt the displayed name and the automatic primary key.

155

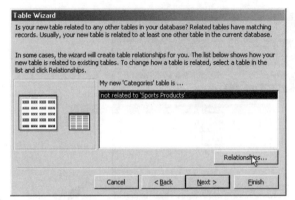

6 Now you get to a new step, as this table could be linked to an existing table. Click on the *Relationships* button, ...

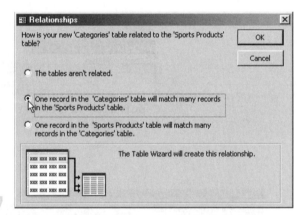

7 ... and define the appropriate type of relationship. As each product category will be applicable to many data records, choose the second option.

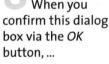

8 When you confirm this dialog box via the *OK* button, ...

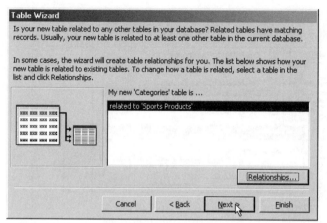

9 ... the new link is added. You can proceed to the next step.

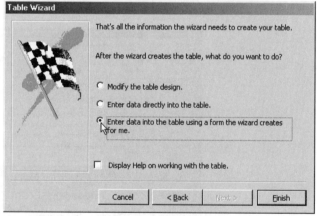

10 The table is complete! You can also create an entry form for the categories at the same time.

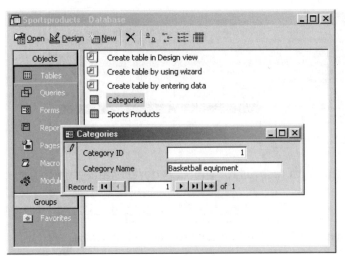

11 Immediately start with the first category. Enter the name and press the ⏎ key to get to the next data record (see the list below).

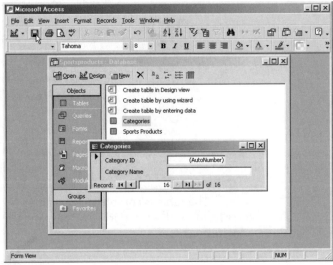

12 Once you have recorded all the data records, save the form.

13 Adopt the suggestion, and close the Form window.

These are the data records for the 'Categories' table, which you can enter in the form:

No.	Category
1	Basketball equipment
2	Football equipment
3	Tennis equipment
4	Balls, general
5	Protection
6	Table tennis
7	Golf equipment
8	Tennis clothing
9	Football clothing
10	Clothing, general
11	Sports footwear
12	Training equipment
13	Inline skating
14	Skateboards
15	Cycling

159

Relational links

The two tables, *Sports Products* and *Categories,* have been relationally linked by the Wizard. The prerequisites were as follows:

↦ A field with the *CategoryID* name and the *Number* field data type in the *Sports Products* table.

↦ A Primary Key field in the *Categories* table with the *CategoryID* name.

Examine the relationship between the two tables with the TOOLS/ RELATIONSHIPS menu command:

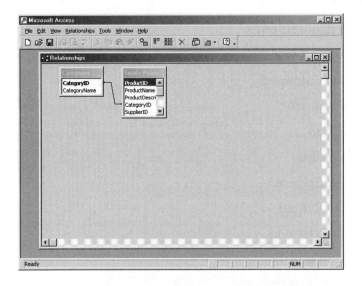

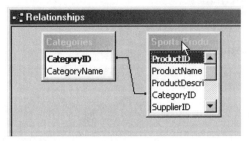

Place the mouse pointer in the Title bar of one of the field lists shown.

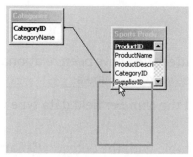

2 Drag the window in any direction.

3 You can enlarge the window using the frame.

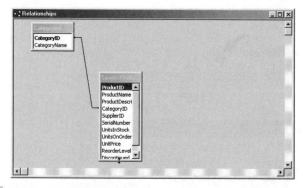

4 Holding down the mouse button, drag the frame downwards.

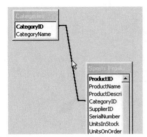

5 Select the line linking the two windows by clicking on it.

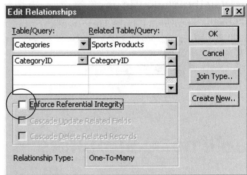

Edit Relationships ? X

Table/Query:	Related Table/Query:	
Categories ▼	Sports Products ▼	OK
CategoryID ▼	CategoryID ▲	Cancel
		Join Type..
	▼	Create New..

☐ Enforce Referential Integrity
☐ Cascade Update Related Fields
☐ Cascade Delete Related Records

Relationship Type: One-To-Many

6 You can get information about the link type by double-clicking on the line.

OK
Cancel
Join Type..

7 Close the window after you have activated 'Referential Integrity'.

8 Now close the Relationships windows, too.

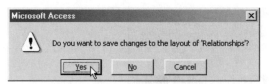

9 Confirm the saving of the changed layout.

Referential Integrity means that the data must not be deleted or modified, if linked information is endangered by it. For example, you would not be allowed to delete category numbers from the *Categories* table, as long as it still exists in the *Sports Products* table.

Table no. 3: Suppliers

Create a further table in your sports products database, which lists all suppliers. When you use the Table Wizard, you can find such a table with fields in the template list. Please note that the Supplier field must be linked relationally to the Supplier Number from the *Sports Products* table. The *Categories* table is not linked to the *Suppliers* table.

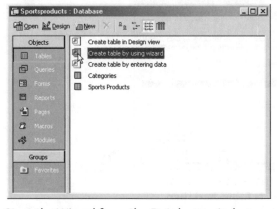

1 Start the Wizard from the Database window.

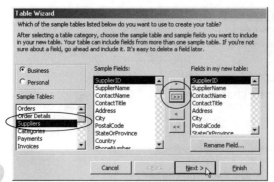

2 Look for the prepared *Suppliers* table and adopt all the fields in the design. Then click on *Next*.

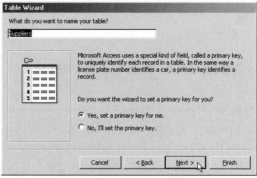

3 Like every other table, this one should also contain a primary key.

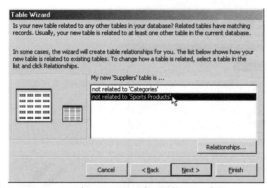

4 Now you need to create the relationships. First select the *Sports Products* table, and then choose the *Relationships* button.

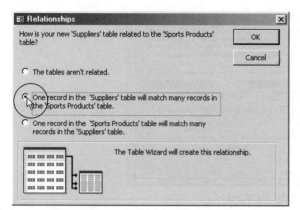

5 This is a 1:n relationship between the Supplier (1) and the Products (n) table.

6 Confirm the link, ...

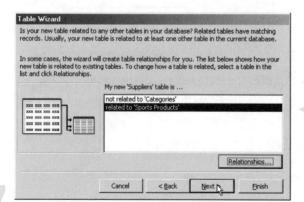

7 ... and let the Wizard prepare a data entry form, too.

165

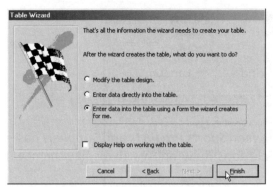

8 Now the table can be created.

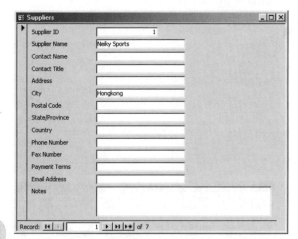

9 Enter the data records of the table below into the form, and then save it.

Here is the data records for the *Suppliers* table:

Supplier's Name	City
Neiky Sports	Hongkong
Roebuck Sportswear	Los Angeles
Bedidas	Paris
Pumela Sport	Munich

Supplier's Name	City
The Trekking Company	Leeds
Kamel Sportsware & Trekking	London
Windermere Sportswear	Windermere

If the relational link between *Sports Products* and *Suppliers* has been entered correctly, the Relationship window will display the new link.

1 Check the window by calling up the TOOLS/ RELATIONSHIPS menu command.

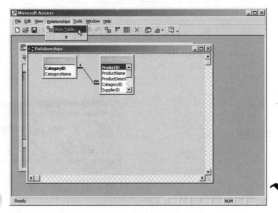

2 The new table is not yet visible. It has to be inserted into the window first.

167

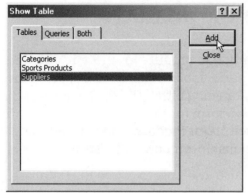

3 Mark *Suppliers* and insert the table into the window.

4 Now you can close the dialog box, ...

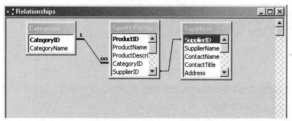

5 ... and the new link will be displayed.

6 Save and close the Relationships window.

An AutoForm for the products

You have come across an option to produce forms more quickly when you were creating the *Categories* table: in the last step, the Wizard offers you the possibility of opening either the Design View or the Data Sheet View, or of using a form for the latter. When you confirm this option, a new unsaved form for the table opens, and you can immediately begin to enter data.

These automatic forms are also available to you in the Database window. This is how to create a quick form for the product data:

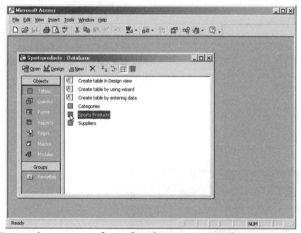

1 To produce a new form for the *Sports Products* table, select the table in the Database window.

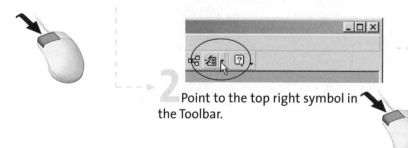

2 Point to the top right symbol in the Toolbar.

169

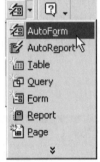

3 Clicking on the small black triangle opens a list of objects that can be created with it.

4 Choose the *AutoForm* option.

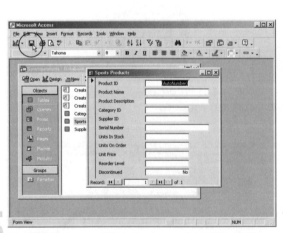

5 The form is immediately created for the table without any further need for confirmation. You can now ...

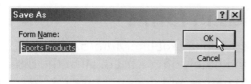

6 ... save it under a suitable name.

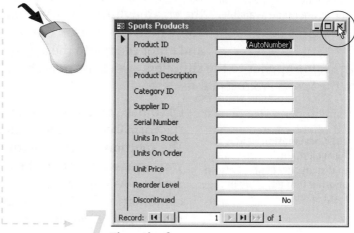

7 Close the form.

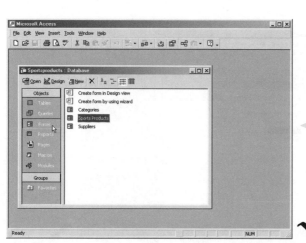

8 Check the Form module in the Database window, which should now display an additional entry.

171

Combination fields in forms

WHAT IS THIS?

The **Toolbox** is a small Toolbar on the left-hand side of the Form design, in which the design tools for forms are made available.

There is one problem: *AutoForm* may immediately offer a list of all of the table's field names, but does not take into account any links to other tables. If, for example, you wish to record the product categories with the created *AutoForm*, you would have to know their numbers in the *Categories* table and enter them into the appropriate field.

The same applies to the suppliers, which are only listed as numbers in the *Sports Products* table.

WHAT IS THIS?

The **Combination field** is a form element, which is able to display any contents from another (linked) table in the form of a list.

Of course you do not want this. However, the Form Design is prepared for this task. The solution is a combination field, which you can create with the help of the Toolbox. As it is not easy to create such a combination field, there is another Wizard to help you with this task.

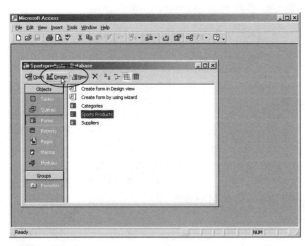

1 Open the Sports Products form from the Database window.

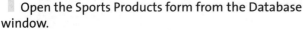

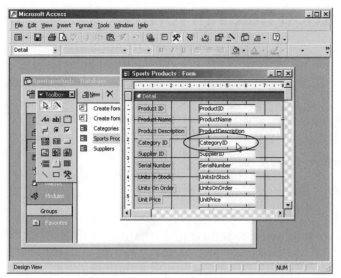

2 The individual form elements are now visible. The Toolbar is on the left-hand side. Select the text field that contains the category ID.

3 Delete the selected field with the Del key.

4 The element and its label have been deleted.

173

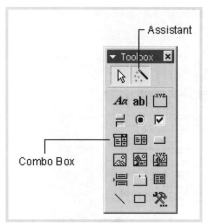

Assistant

Combo Box

5 Now activate the *Combination Field* tool. Please note that the Wizard must be switched on, too.

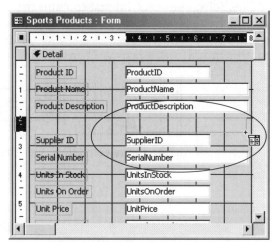

6 Place the mouse pointer, which turns into crosshairs, on the point at which you want the field to begin. Drag open a rectangle until it has the appropriate size. Do not forget to keep pressing the mouse button during this process.

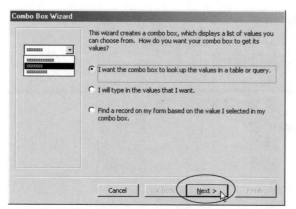

7 The field is now going to be created.
The Wizard starts.

The Wizard is now going to take you step by step through the creation of the new field. First, it asks you whether the field refers to values from another table (in this case: yes, namely from the *Categories* table). Thus you can confirm the first step straightaway.

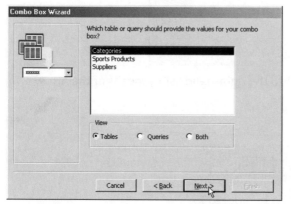

1 Here the table has already been correctly selected. You can click on *Next*.

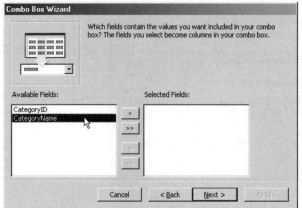

In the next step you need to specify what you want
to have included from the other table in your form. Select
Category Name, ...

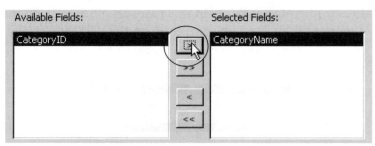

... and copy it to the right-hand list by means of the Arrow symbol.

Click on *Next* to proceed to
the next step, ...

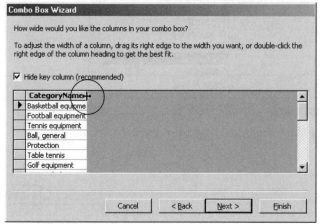

5 ... which displays the new field. Now you need to specify the correct width. Double-click on the right-hand column line to adjust the column width.

6 Click on *Next*.

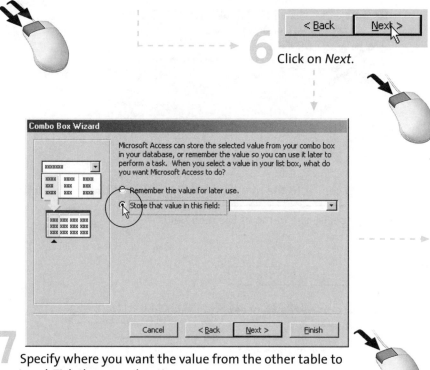

7 Specify where you want the value from the other table to be stored. Tick the second option, ...

177

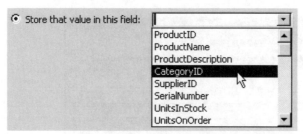

8 ... and choose the *CategoryID* field from the list.

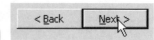

9 Proceed to the final step of the Wizard.

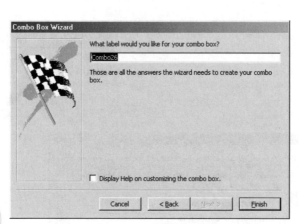

10 Finally, specify the name of the new field.

11 Enter the name, ...

12 ... and finish the Wizard.

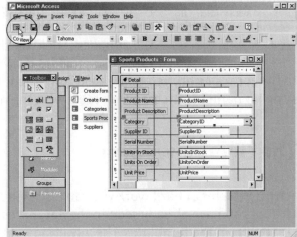

13 The new field on the form is complete. You can now switch to data entry.

14 The combination field now provides the categories from the *Categories* table. The chosen category number will be saved.

TIP

Which field must contain the value that is provided by the combination field? Of course, the *SupplierID* field.

Have you managed to do everything? This technique is not easy, but is part of the practice of designing forms as much as relationships are part of a relational database. Immediately try the whole procedure again: the *SupplierID* field on the Sports Products form also provides only numbers. Switch back to the Form Design, delete the field from the form, and extract the supplier names from the other table with the help of the Wizard.

The Overview form

With a little bit of hard work you can also create an Overview form such as you have already seen in the databases the Wizard has created from the templates. The advantage of the form: all tables, forms, and reports are available to you at the touch of a button and you do not have to look for them in the Database window.

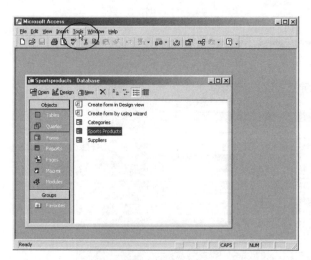

1 In the *Tools* menu look for the *Switchboard* menu command.

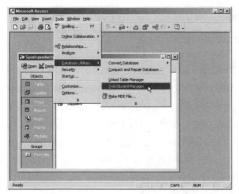

2 Here a manager is provided for this. Start it, ...

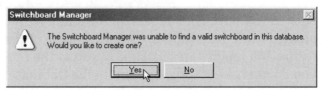

3 ... and confirm the creation of a new Overview with the *Yes* button (later on you can also modify the overview using this option).

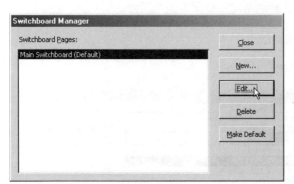

4 The switchboard contains the buttons for forms and reports.

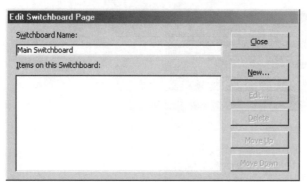

5 Change the Overview name, which actually is just a form.

6 Then start with the first entry.

New...

7 Enter the text that will be visible in the overview form into the first field.

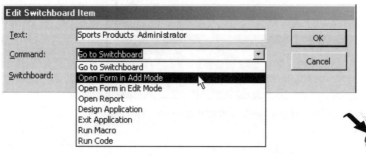

8 Enter the description of the Product Management form, and choose the appropriate command for it.

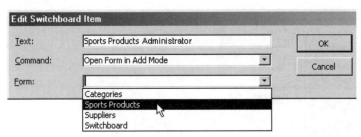

9 Now only the form itself is missing; pick it from the drop-down list in the third entry box.

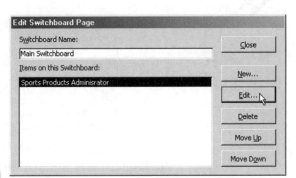

10 You have now finished the first entry on the Overview form. Pick the other two forms in the same way as entries with the *Open Form in Add Mode* command.

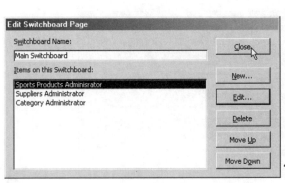

11 Now the manager has all details it requires for the Overview form. Close both windows.

 12 You can either open the Overview manually, ...

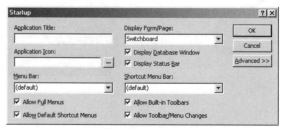

13 .... or specify under TOOLS/STARTUP that you want this form to open automatically at the start-up of the database.

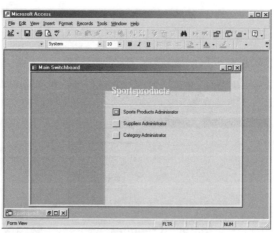

14 From now on your database starts with the Overview form.

A brief checklist

Please take the time to work through this exercise. Simply answer the questions with *Right* or *Wrong*.

Statement	Right	Wrong
1. File names can consist of up to 255 characters.		
2. The slash is allowed in file names.		
3. Table fields that are suggested by the Table Wizard must always be adopted.		
4. The Table Wizard field names can be renamed.		
5. Tables cannot be linked relationally without a primary key.		
6. The field data type of the primary key is always Text.		
7. The relational links between tables cannot be made visible.		
8. In the Relationships window, you can view the exact links when you click on a line.		
9. Referential Integrity ensures that you cannot delete data still used in other tables.		
10. By means of combination fields, the form can display data from other tables.		
11. The Overview is a form that can be entered into the Start form.		

Answers to this checklist are to be found in the Appendix.

A personal birthdays database

What's in this chapter?

You have always wanted to record the birthdays of your friends, relations, and colleagues so that you will never forget them again. Furthermore, you will have to filter tables by specific criteria, and for this you prefer to use queries. In this chapter you are going to create a list of the names and birthdays of staff members and colleagues, and analyse it with the help of various queries.

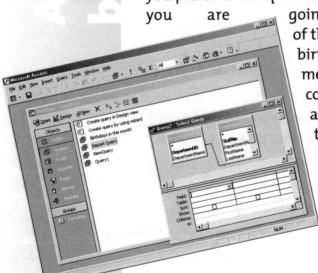

The table for your colleagues' data

Of course, you can also use the general Address database or any general database, in which the names of colleagues, friends, and so on are saved, as the basis of this database. We are going to create a new database and in it the tables with relational links, using the Table Wizard:

1 After the start-up of Access 2000 (from the Start menu), activate the first option for a new database.

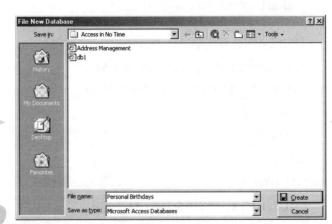

2 Enter the name of the new MDB file, ...

3 ... and create the new database.

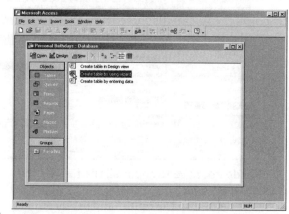

4 In the Database window begin with the first table. Generate its structure with the Table Wizard.

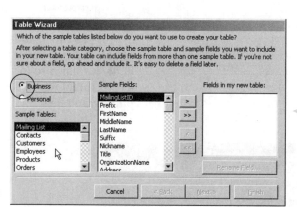

5 In the Table Wizard select the category *Business*, where you can find a great selection of Table Designs.

6 Activate the Design *Employees*.

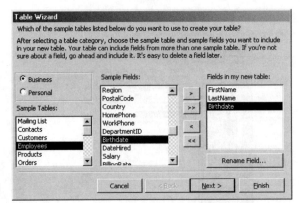

7 You do not have to adopt all the fields. Only click on those which are included in the above list. Copy the fields into the right-hand list by double-clicking on them.

8 If you can include photographs of your staff in file format, also include a corresponding photograph field.

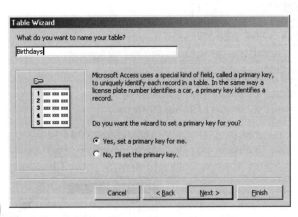

9 Now enter a distinctive name for the table, ...

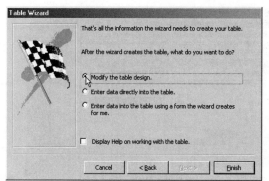

10 ... and the table is almost complete. Check the design again by selecting the *Modify the table design* radio button.

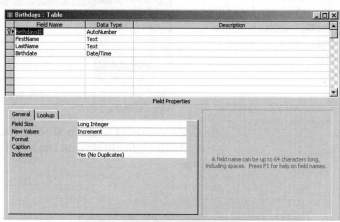

11 This is what the table looks like in Design View.

The **OLE object** is part of the data record, which has been produced by a different program, a so-called OLE server. Images from Corel Draw, videos, or sound files are all examples of OLE objects for which there is a separate data type in the field structure.

Unfortunately the Wizard could not recognise the purpose of the division number, and has made it the Primary Key field. You have to do something about this:

Primary Key symbol

1 First delete the primary key by clicking on the Primary Key symbol. Then change the data type of the field to *Number* with the field size *Long Integer*. Save the structure.

2 Now insert a new first row. Open the context menu by right clicking on the left-hand edge of the row.

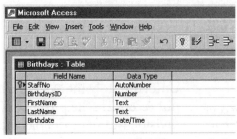

3 Enter the field name *StaffNo* into the new row. Apply the *AutoNumber* data type to the field, then click on the Key symbol to assign the primary key to it. Save the modified structure and then close the window.

The linked department list

A second table is going to contain the department names. With a relational link you are going to ensure that the department number from the first table is also the number from the second. Use the Table Wizard. It will suggest the type of link. Create the new table with the Database window:

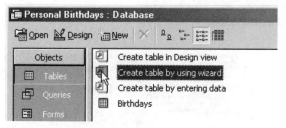

1 Use the Table Wizard again.

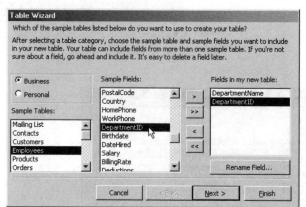

2 Pick the *DepartmentID* and *DepartmentName* fields from the same table as before.

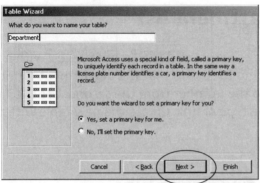

3 The name indicates that the table is a Department list.

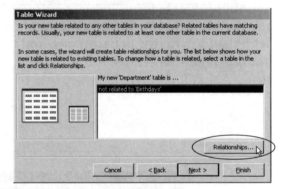

4 Determine the relationship between the two tables in the next step.

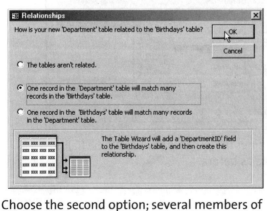

5 Choose the second option; several members of staff may work in one department.

The rest is already a matter of routine to you: save the table; close the design; and check the relationship under TOOLS/ RELATIONS to make sure.

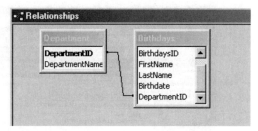

Creating forms for the tables

You should create forms for data entry. However, because of the relational link between the tables you need to modify them. Begin with the form for the departments, and then create the form for the staff members. Instead of the entry field for the department number insert a combination field, which lists the department names.

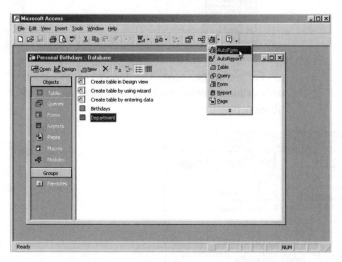

Create an AutoForm for the *Department* table from the Database window.

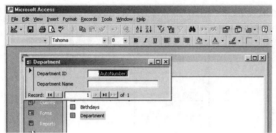

2 Immediately save the new form under the suggested name.

3 For a change create the second form with the Form Wizard. Switch to the Form module, and click on the *New* button.

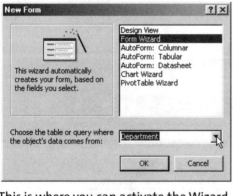

4 This is where you can activate the Wizard. Do not forget to choose the table to which the form refers from the list below.

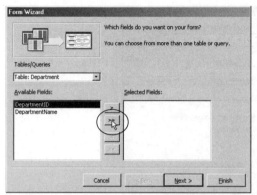

5 The next step offers you the option to select individual fields. We require all the fields, therefore click on the double arrow.

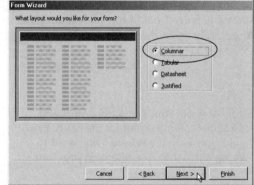

6 Now you only have to sort out the layout of the form. In this case the single column layout is the most useful.

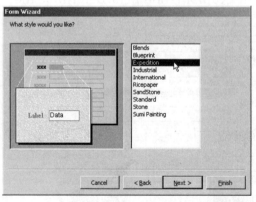

7 The next dialog box offers ready-made styles (font, background, and colours). Choose a style.

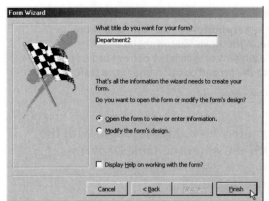

8 This is the final step of the Wizard. You can display the Form Design for modifications or immediately open the form to start entering data.

Check your knowledge of linked tables and Combination Fields: the field for the department numbers is substituted by a Combination Field that does not offer the numbers but the department names. Delete the field *DepartmentID* and draw in a combination field. Determine the relationship to the *Staff* table with the Wizard. The field contents are again saved in the field *DepartmentID*.

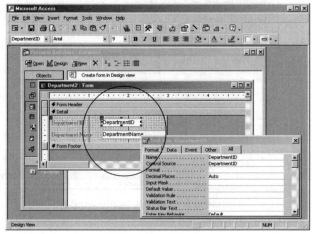

The new field is located at the very bottom of the form and is the last field you enter data into. With the menu command VIEW/ CUSTOM ORDER you can open a window in which the current order is displayed. Drag the field into the second position under the staff number.

Now you can enter data into your database. Begin with the Department list, in which you enter the table *Department*:

Department No.	Department Name
1	Purchasing Department
2	Sales Department
3	Administration
4	EDP/Customer Service
5	Production
6	Warehouse/Shipping Department
7	Personnel

Record the staff members with the newly created form, which also offers the department in a combination field:

No.	Department	First Name	Name	Birthday
1	Purchasing Department	John	Herriott	12.1.70
2	Purchasing Department	Darren	Morris	15.3.74
3	Purchasing Department	Sarah	Farrow	21.7.72
4	Purchasing Department	Lisa	Edwards	3.11.77
5	Sales Department	Barry	Smith	29.3.75
6	Sales Department	Richard	Shaw	14.9.50
7	Sales Department	Rachel	Fox	26.7.56
8	Production	Robert	Cavendish	3.6.58
9	Production	Leanne	Ellis	12.6.52
10	Production	Lorraine	Humphreys	16.1.62
11	Production	Monica	Coleman	5.7.62

The first query

A **query** stores information about the number of data records and the selection of the fields that are to be displayed in table format. A query is generated once and then saved. The saved query can then be run with the current data of one or more tables at any time.

You want to produce a simple list of all members of staff in all divisions. As this information is distributed across two tables you need to run a query. Use the Query Wizard. It will provide you with a quick result.

1 In the Database window choose the Query module, and start the first query.

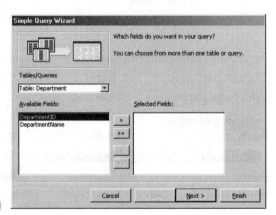

2 The Query Wizard is activated, ...

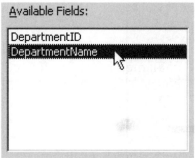

3 ... and the list displays the
fields of the table which is
specified above. Mark
DepartmentName, ...

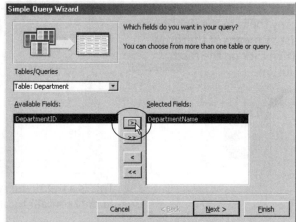

4 ... and copy it to the right into the field list. We do
not require the department number.

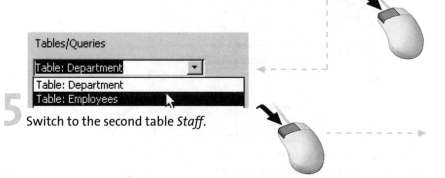

5 Switch to the second table *Staff*.

201

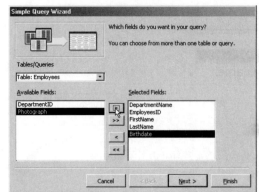

6 From this table we only require the fields shown. Mark them individually and copy them to the right-hand list by means of the arrow. Then click on the *Next* button.

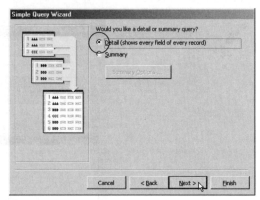

7 This is a Detail query; a Summary query would only contain totals and similar items.

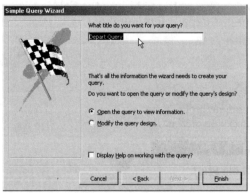

8 In the next step you are offered a query name. Immediately overtype the suggestion ...

What title do you want for your query?

Depart Query

9 ... with the above query name.

Finish

10 Now you can finish the query.

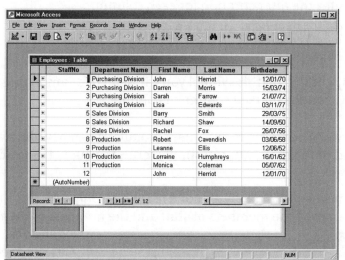

StaffNo	Department Name	First Name	Last Name	Birthdate
1	Purchasing Division	John	Herriot	12/01/70
2	Purchasing Division	Darren	Morris	15/03/74
3	Purchasing Division	Sarah	Farrow	21/07/72
4	Purchasing Division	Lisa	Edwards	03/11/77
5	Sales Division	Barry	Smith	29/03/75
6	Sales Division	Richard	Shaw	14/09/50
7	Sales Division	Rachel	Fox	26/07/56
8	Production	Robert	Cavendish	03/06/58
9	Production	Leanne	Ellis	12/06/52
10	Production	Lorraine	Humphreys	16/01/62
11	Production	Monica	Coleman	05/07/62
12		John	Herriot	12/01/70
(AutoNumber)				

11 And this is the result: a list of the members of staff and their departments.

It is very easy to rearrange the column order in the query result. Mark a column by clicking on the column header. Holding down the mouse button in this position drag the column between two other columns.

You can now go on to edit or print out the table. Sort or filter it with the symbols on the toolbar, or hide individual columns.

 With this symbol you can sort the query in descending order by the marked column.

 Use this button to sort the query in ascending order.

 Clicking on this symbol filters the query by the marked criterion (for example, department name).

 With this button you can generate a form in which you can enter the filter criterion for each column.

 This icon removes all the filters in the query.

 By clicking on this symbol you can search for any expression within the marked column or columns.

The query will be stored in the Query module. When new data records are added to the table, you can simply rerun the query to include the new records.

Create a new query, namely a phone list, which only contains the family names of the members of staff and the numbers of their extensions.

Activate the Query wizard and collect the fields from the two tables. Save the query under *Staff Phone List*.

Editing queries

In practice, queries which have been created with the help of the Wizard are usually only used at the beginning. Only you can generate the right kind of query in the Query window. Only the Query window offers you all the options to analyse your data. Produce and edit the next query in the Query window.

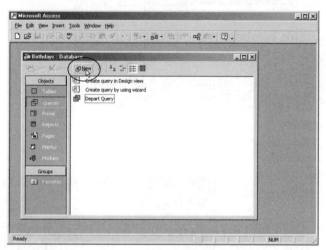

Switch to the Database window and into the Query module for the next query. Click on the *New* button.

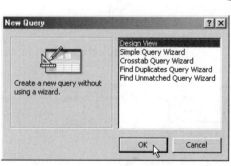

Now choose the Design View.

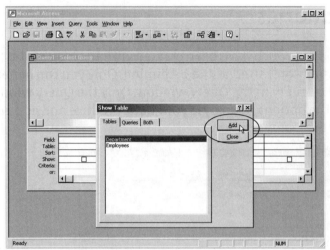

3 The query is created immediately. All the tables from the Table module are on offer. Insert the first table.

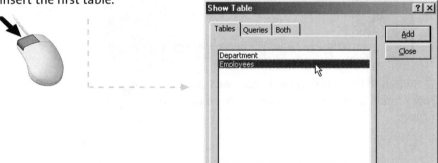

4 Mark the second table, ...

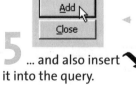

5 ... and also insert it into the query.

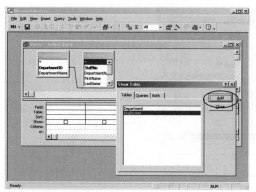

6 Now you have inserted all the tables involved in the query. You can close the Table list.

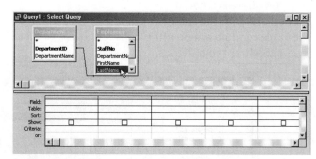

7 You want the first column to display the family name. Mark it in the field list, ...

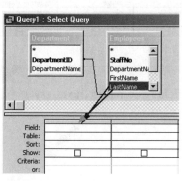

8 ... and, pressing the mouse button, drag it into the query area.

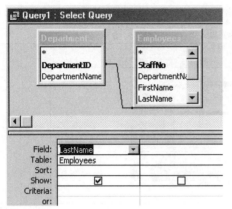

9 The field is inserted as soon as you release the mouse button.

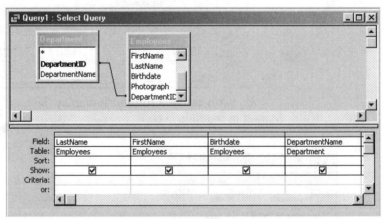

10 In the same way drag all the fields down into the query area in the appropriate order.

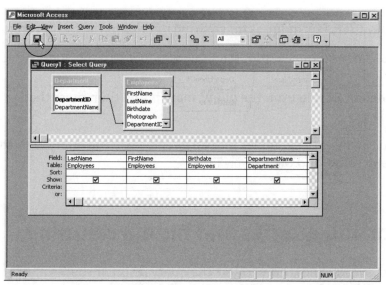

So far the query is complete, and you can save it, ...

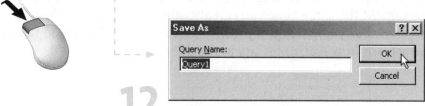

... assign a suitable name, ...

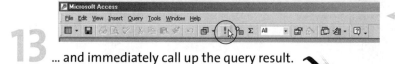

... and immediately call up the query result.

Very large field lists can quickly be inserted into the query: double-click on the title bar of the field list. This automatically marks all the fields, and you can drag the marked block down with the mouse.

209

A few useful techniques for creating queries in the Design window:

➡ You can send tables from the Table window into the query by double clicking on them.

➡ To delete a table from the query, mark it and then press the ⌦ key.

➡ You can insert new tables into an already existing query with the menu command QUERY/SHOW TABLE.

Sorting queries and hiding columns

You already know how to sort the query result. If you want your query to produce already sorted results, you have to integrate the specification of the sorting type and the sorting field into the Query Design. At the same time you can also hide unnecessary columns. This is particularly important if you do not want to display linked fields which are, however, necessary in the query.

Open an existing query in Design View.

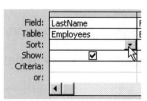

2 Apart from a field name each column also has a sorting field. Place the cursor into this row, open the list, ...

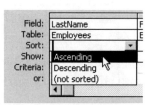

3 ... and choose the appropriate sorting type for this field.

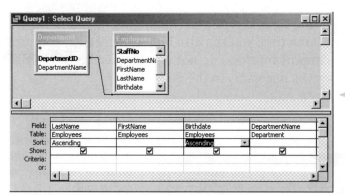

4 Now the query will be sorted by this field. You can specify further fields.

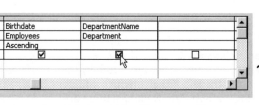

5 Remove the tick from the *Show* row if you want to hide a column.

6 With this symbol you can also view the query result.

7 Save the modified query under a new name with the FILE/SAVE AS menu command.

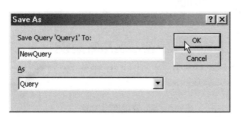

8 Enter a name for the new query.

How are the **query fields sorted** if more than one sorting field has been specified? They are sorted by the field that is furthest to the left. If this column contains identical entries (for example, family names) these are sorted by the next field, and so on.

Filtering queries by criteria

A further option to edit queries is offered by the *Criteria* row. Here you can filter the query by the specified criterion. This may be an individual field entry such as a department name or a complex formula.

Now create a query that displays only the staff of a particular department:

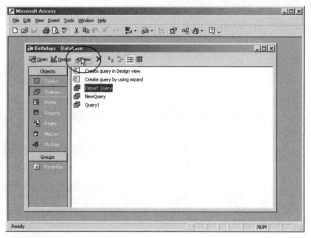

Start the next query in the Database window.

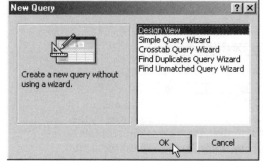

Again choose the *Design View*.

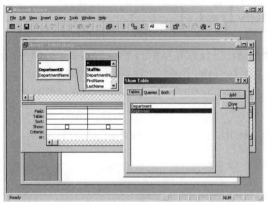

3 Add the two tables, and close the Table window.

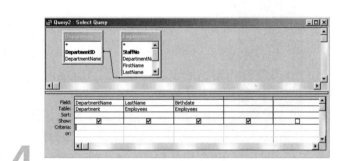

4 Drag the three field names into the query, and place the cursor into the Criteria row of the first column.

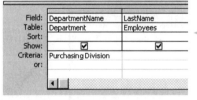

5 Enter a department name.

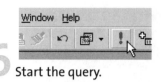

6 Start the query.

Query2 : Select Query			
Department Name	Last Name	Birthdate
▶ Purchasing Department	Herriot	12/01/70
Purchasing Department	Morris	15/03/74
Purchasing Department	Farrow	21/07/72
Purchasing Department	Edwards	03/11/77
*		

Record: I◀ ◀ | 1 | ▶ ▶I ▶* of 4

7 It now shows only the data records that comply with this criterion.

You can use logical operators such as *AND* and *OR. BETWEEN, NOT,* and *LIKE* are also permitted. You may also enter logical signs such as >= (greater than or equal to).

The table below lists a few examples of criteria in queries:

Field	Criterion	Meaning
Department	"Purchasing Department" OR "Sales"	All data records which contain either of the departments.
Department	NOT "Production"	All departments apart from Production.
Name	LIKE "S*"	All names which begin with S.

Begin your next query, which will be used as the basis of the monthly Birthday Report. In this report all members of staff are listed whose birthday falls in the current month.

215

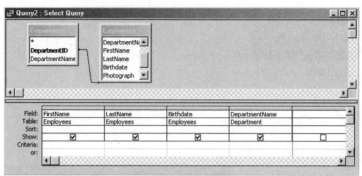

1 You can use an already existing query or create a new one with these fields.

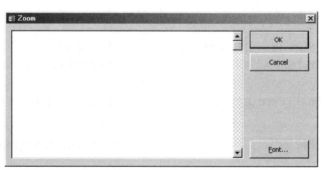

2 Place the cursor into the Criteria field of the Birthday column.

3 With ⇧+F2 you open the Zoom window in which you can enter the formula.

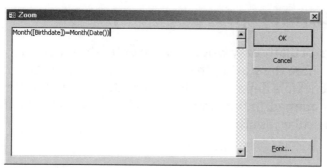

4 Enter this formula. It compares the month of the Birthday field with that of the current date.

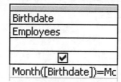

5 The formula is adopted into the Criteria field, ...

6 ... and when you start the query, ...

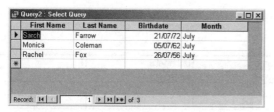

7 ... it only shows the staff members whose birthday falls in the current month.

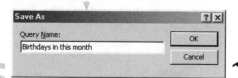

6 Save the query under the name shown above by clicking on the Diskette symbol on the toolbar.

217

The Parameter query

Querying is particularly easy when you can enter the criterion immediately before the start of the query. In this way you can create, for example, a flexible department list, in which the appropriate department is queried. In this way you can also produce the Birthday List of any particular month.

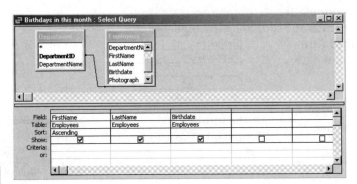

1 Reactivate the query you have just created and remove the formula from the Criteria row.

2 First calculate the month of the birthday in the empty column next to the last field. With ⇧+F2 you get into the Zoom window.

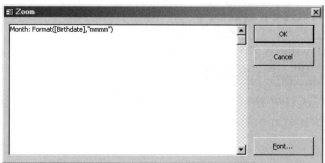

3 Enter this formula. It determines the month of the field Birthday by means of the *Format* instruction.

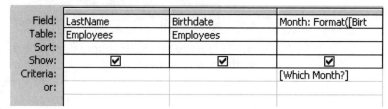

Field:	LastName	Birthdate	Month: Format([Birt
Table:	Employees	Employees	
Sort:			
Show:	☑	☑	☑
Criteria:			[Which Month?]
or:			

4 In the Criteria row insert the question required for the Parameter query in square brackets.

Query   Tools   Window   Help

5 Start the query, ...

219

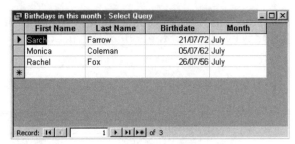

6 ... and enter the appropriate month.

7 This is the result: the query filters the data records by the parameter entered.

Remember to save the new query under a new name with the FILE/SAVE AS menu command.

A brief checklist

Test your knowledge. This exercise will help you to revise and reinforce what you have learnt so far. Match the ten expressions in the first table to the explanations that follow below.

A ⇧ + F2

B Toolbox

C OLE object

D   LIKE "A*"

E   QUERY/SHOW TABLE

F   Parameter query

G   Criterion

H   Activation series

I   Query

J   Sorting

Match these definitions with the above expressions.

1.   This is the field data type for image data (for example, photographs).

2.   This is the name of the toolbar that contains the tools for Combination fields.

3.   This option in the VIEW menu is used to arrange form fields correctly.

4.   If you need more than one table for a form you have to create one of these.

5.   You need this option in the Form Design if a table is missing.

6.   This can be found to the extreme left of the row in the Query Design, which sorts the data records alphabetically.

7.   This is the term that is used to refer to the instruction in a query that filters the result.

8.   With this criterion the query can extract all the fields that begin with A.

9.   This is what you press if you want to view the formula in the Zoom window.

10.   This is what queries that ask you in advance what you want them to filter are called.

You can find the answers to this small checklist in the Appendix.

The Shareware Archive

What's in this chapter:

The outputting of data records in reports
is the main topic of this practical example.
You should already be familiar with the
report as the output medium of the
database. With the help of the Wizards it
can be produced quickly. In this chapter you
are also going to learn how to adapt it to
your requirements, for example to print
labels. To revise already learnt techniques
you are going to
create a relational
database with links
and a query.

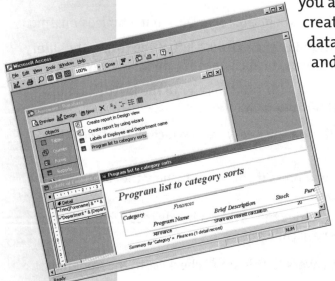

Creating database tables

Just like every workshop example in this book this one also starts with a lot of work: to begin you have to design the database, and this means first the tables and then the relational links between them. Our task is to create a Shareware Archive, which can be used by members of staff. The members of staff can borrow the programs for testing. To ensure that we do not lose track of the transactions, an overview of all the transactions with date borrowed, program description, and return date is kept.

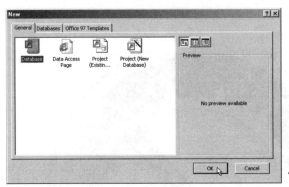

1 Create a new MDB file with the FILE/NEW menu command.

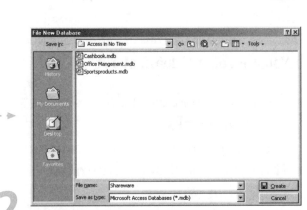

2 Name the new file.

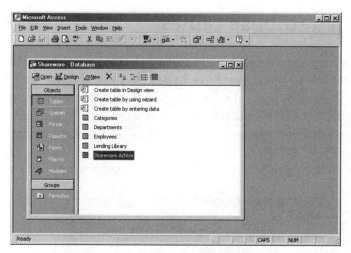

3 These are the tables in the Table module, which are required for the database model. Start with the Shareware Archive. First create this table.

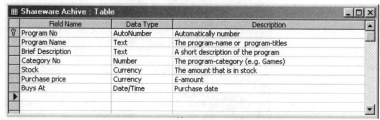

4 As Category designate a link in the form of a Number field. All the remaining fields are standard.

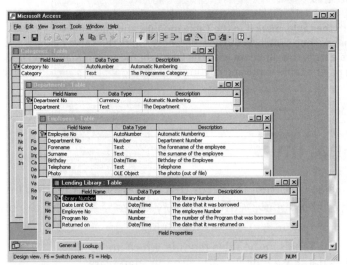

5   Here are the designs of the remaining tables, which you can also copy from the database we created in the preceding chapter (see below).

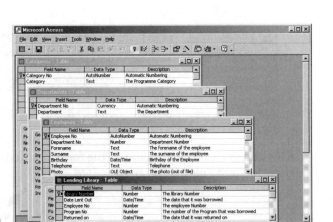

6   This is the Leanding Library, which contains links to the Staff table and the Shareware Archive.

You can simply copy the tables from the already existing databases: open the database with the table, mark it in the Table module, and choose the EDIT/COPY menu command. Then switch to the new database, mark the Table module, and insert the table from the clipboard with the EDIT/PASTE menu command. You now only need to enter a table name and confirm that you adopt the structure and the data.

Relational links

Now you have to link the tables. For this purpose a connecting line is drawn from each window with a primary key to the field in the other table which has been reserved for the field.

You can understand that literally, since links are forged in exactly this way in the Relationship window.

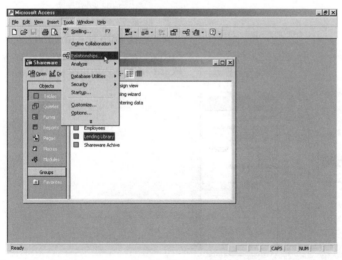

1 Open the Relationship window from the Tools menu.

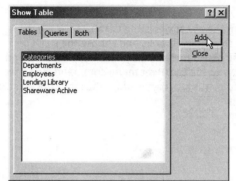

2 Insert all the tables from the Table module into the window. Double-clicking on an entry immediately copies it into the window.

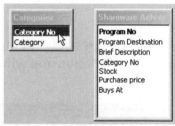

3 Start with the link between *Categories* and *Shareware Archive*. Point to the Primary Key field.

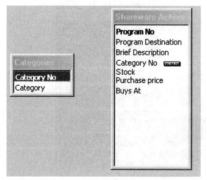

4 Holding down the mouse button drag it into the *Shareware Archive* table. Release the mouse button as soon as the field is above the corresponding field you want to link it to.

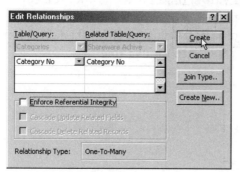

5 The linked field appears. Confirm your entry.

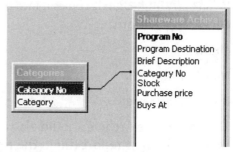

6 The result: a connecting line indicates the relational relationship between the two tables.

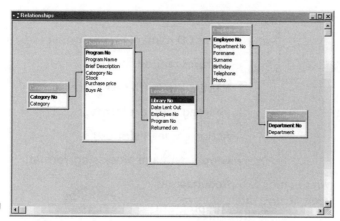

7 And this is what the network of relationships looks like once you have inserted all the connecting lines.

Now only the data for the individual tables are missing. You can enter them on the data sheets or on the forms, which you create as AutoForms that possess combination fields for the linked data fields. Below are the data records for the Categories table:

- Games
- Utilities
- Operating system
- Graphics/CAD
- Foreign languages
- Office applications
- Finances
- Music/video
- Internet/intranet

The Shareware Archive should also contain a few test data before you produce the first report (fill in the remaining columns as you like):

Program Name	Brief Description
Translator XXX	Translation program
AllFinance	Share and interest calculation
DisC-Play	Music CD management Graphics Texture
Collection	Textures for designers
HTML Light	HTML editor with text processor
Internet Phone	Phoning via the Internet
Conquistador	Action game (historical)
Paint Shop Pro	Graphics, image processing, formats
Monster Truck	Action game
Picture Publisher	DTP program
Proverbs and quotations	Dictionary of proverbs and quotations

Creating a query for the program list

To create a first report that contains all programs from the Shareware Archive, you need a query. The *Shareware Archive* table alone is not enough as the basis for the report, since it only contains the category numbers and not the category names of the individual items.

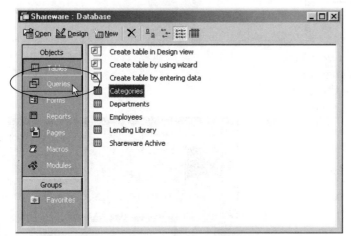

In the Database window switch to the Query module and create a new query.

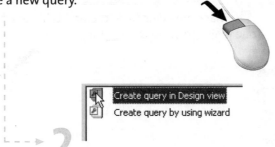

The quickest way of doing this is in Design View.

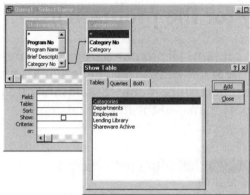

3 Insert the two tables *Shareware Archive* and *Categories* into the query by double-clicking on them. Then close the Table window.

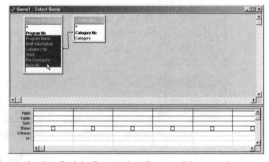

4 Mark the fields from the first table one by one while pressing the ⇧ key.

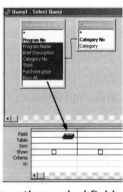

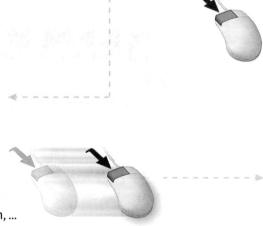

5 Drag the marked fields downward into the first column, ...

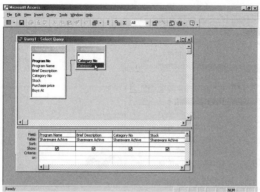

6 ... and release the mouse button.
The fields of the first table are now in
the query. Copy the *Category* field from
the second table into the last column by
double-clicking on it.

7 Save the query, ...

8 ... and enter a name for it.

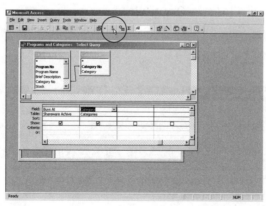

9 The first query in the Query module of the Database window
can now be called up with the Exclamation Mark symbol.

Programs and categories : Select Query	
Program Name	**Brief D**
Translator XXX	Translation progra
▶ AllFinance	Share and interes
DisC-Play	Music CD manag
Graphics Texture Collection	Textures for Desi
HTML Light	HTML editor with
Internet Phone	Phoning via the Ir
Conquistador	Action game (hist
Paint Shop Pro	Graphics, image
Monster Truck	Action game
Picture Publisher	DTP program
Proverbs and quotations	Dictioary of prove

10 Optimally adjust the width of the individual columns by double-clicking on the line between the column headings.

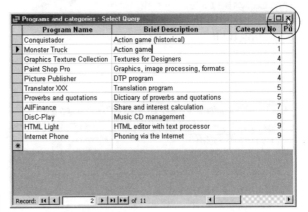

Programs and categories : Select Query			
Program Name	**Brief Description**	**Category No**	**Pu**
Conquistador	Action game (historical)	1	
▶ Monster Truck	Action game	1	
Graphics Texture Collection	Textures for Designers	4	
Paint Shop Pro	Graphics, image processing, formats	4	
Picture Publisher	DTP program	4	
Translator XXX	Translation program	5	
Proverbs and quotations	Dictioary of proverbs and quotations	5	
AllFinance	Share and interest calculation	7	
DisC-Play	Music CD management	8	
HTML Light	HTML editor with text processor	9	
Internet Phone	Phoning via the Internet	9	
*			

Record: I◀ ◀ | 2 | ▶ ▶I ▶* of 11

11 Close the Query window, ...

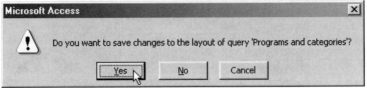

Microsoft Access ✕

⚠ Do you want to save changes to the layout of query 'Programs and categories'?

[Yes] [No] [Cancel]

12 ... and confirm this message which refers to the modification of the column widths.

The first report: a program list

Now it is time for the first report, which will contain a list of the Shareware products from the database. The query, which contains not only the programs but also the categories, has already been created. Therefore we can begin immediately:

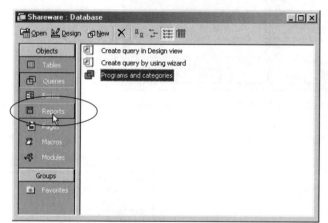

1 First activate the Report module in the Database window for the new report.

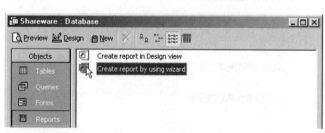

2 Choose the Report Wizard. It will take you to the finished report in the dialog.

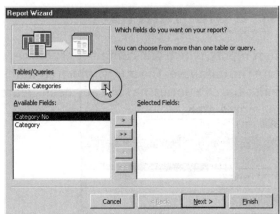

3 The Wizard is active but it offers the wrong table. Open this list, ...

Table: Categories

Table: Categories
Table: Categories
Table: Departments
Table: Employees
Table: Lending Library
Table: Shareware Achive
Query: Programs and categories

4 ... and mark the recently created query.

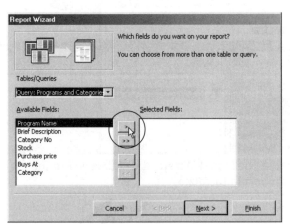

5 Then choose the fields, which should appear in the report. The first field is already marked. Click on the arrow to copy it into the selection list.

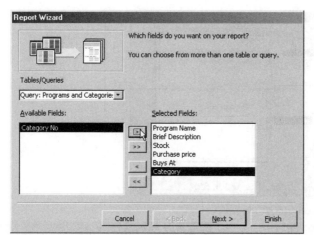

6 Copy all the fields apart from *Category No* into the right-hand list.

In the next step you are going to determine the Grouping field for the report.

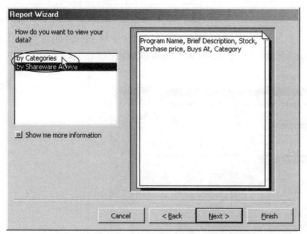

1 Here *Category* appears to be the most suitable option.

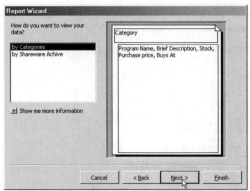

2 The Preview window now shows that under the *Category* field groups of data records are formed. Proceed to the next step.

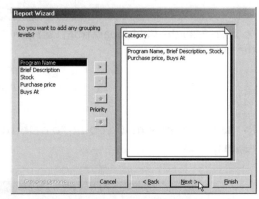

3 Here you can create a further grouping level. However, this is not necessary for our report.

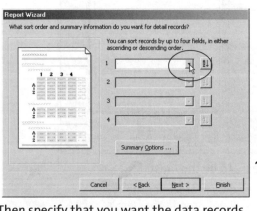

4 Then specify that you want the data records to be sorted in ascending order.

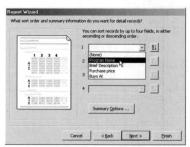

5 The program name is very well suited as a sorting criterion.

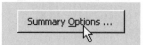

6 Under this button you can find options for report totals and other summaries.

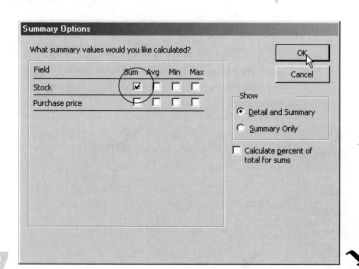

7 Calculate the sum of the items in stock for the individual categories, which will be listed in the detail area and in the summary.

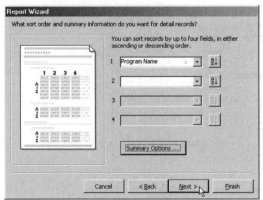

8 Proceed to the next step of the Wizard.

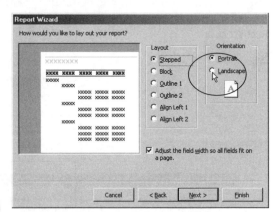

9 The Layout window determines the page setup and the orientation of the data records. Choose *Landscape*.

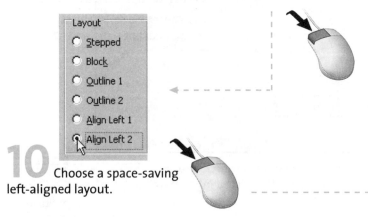

10 Choose a space-saving left-aligned layout.

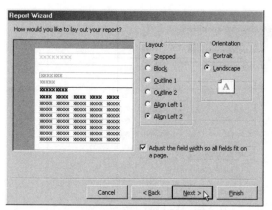

11 The fields are automatically reduced until they all fit onto the page. You can proceed to the next step, ...

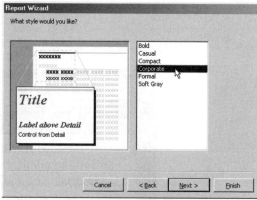

12 ... where you can choose a style. The style determines the colours, fonts, font sizes, and line elements used in the report.

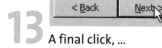

13 A final click, ...

241

14 ... and you can name and finish the report.
Take care to enter a meaningful name in the entry box.

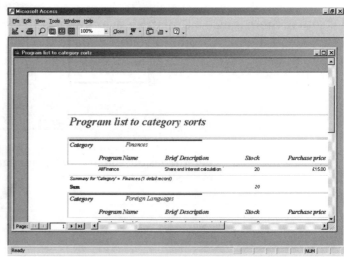

15 After a short period in which the program
calculates the totals the finished report is displayed
with groups and subtotals.

Carefully examine the report. For this purpose you can use the two zoom tools *Zoom Magnifier* and *Zoom Field*:

Zoom Magnifier. Zooms between the set zoom and Full Screen View.

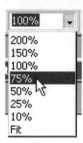

Zoom Field. Choose the suitable zoom factor for your screen.

You can now create further reports with the Report Wizard, for example a staff list sorted by divisions, or a program list sorted by purchase price.

Designing reports

Of course there is also a Design View for reports, in which you can edit every single element, from the report page to the individual fields and to drawing objects such as lines. We are now going to edit the first report directly in design View.

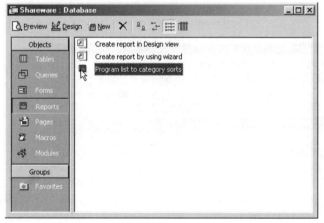

1 Mark the report in the Report module of the Database window, ...

2 ... and open it with the *Design* button.

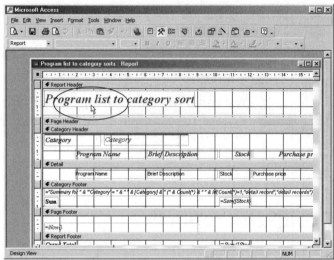

3 This is what the Design looks like. Reports – like forms – are subdivided into areas. For example, when you mark the title element in the report header, ...

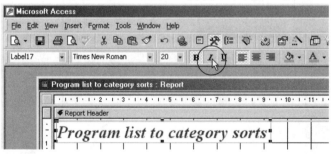

4 ... you can read and edit its formatting in the toolbar (here, for example, deactivate *Italic*).

Have a look at the VIEW menu: here the most important areas Page Header/Footer and Report Header/Footer are offered at the very bottom. You can click on the appropriate command to show or hide the element.

In the Header and Detail area you will need to format (fonts, colours, Italic, Bold, and so on) not only individual elements but usually also the entire row. This is how to select entire rows:

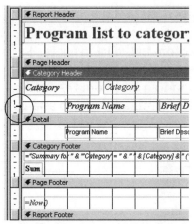

1 To mark an entire row of elements place the mouse pointer on the left-hand edge of the row. The mouse pointer turns into an arrow.

2 When you click with the mouse button all the row elements are marked.

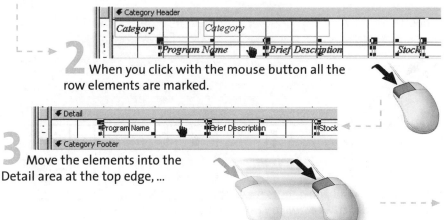

3 Move the elements into the Detail area at the top edge, ...

4 ... and drag the line marking the bottom edge of the area upwards, so that there is no superfluous empty space between the rows.

Formulas in reports

If you scroll the vertical scrollbar to the right and the horizontal scrollbar downward you can make out the formula which inserts the page numbers in the corner at the bottom in the Page Footer. Such formulas can be inserted in every area. You only need a text field, which you can draw with the corresponding tool from the Toolbox. This is how you can find out where the formula is written and what it looks like:

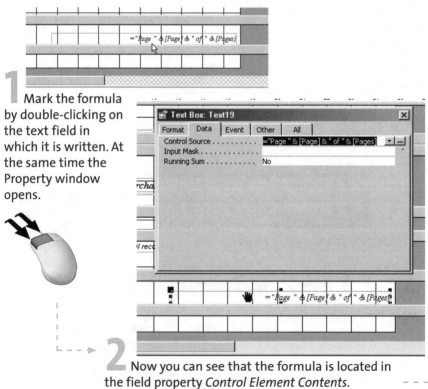

1 Mark the formula by double-clicking on the text field in which it is written. At the same time the Property window opens.

2 Now you can see that the formula is located in the field property *Control Element Contents*.

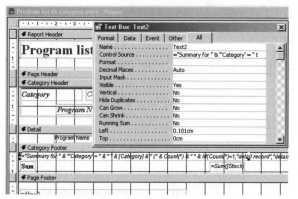

3 Here we see a more complex formula to sum up the category totals.

To make it easier to edit the formula, place the cursor in the Property field and press ⇧ + F2. The Zoom window now offers enough space even for large formulas.

Where does the program store the information about the grouping levels and sorting?
These specifications can be found in a separate window. If you wish you can also delete or add individual groups in this window.

1 Call up the SORTING & GROUPING command in the VIEW menu.

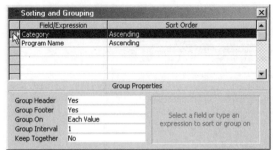

2 The window shows all groupings and sorting. Each row represents a grouping or a sorting.

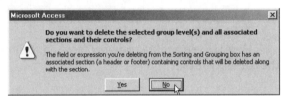

3 When you mark a row and delete it with the [Del] key you will receive a message, which warns you that you will also lose the elements of the grouping.

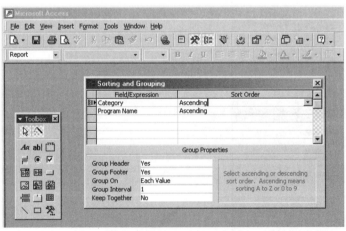

4 The toolbar offers two symbols with which you can activate and deactivate the Toolbox and the SORTING & GROUPING window.

Assigning an AutoFormat

You can format every single area of your report differently. You can either mark the individual elements and then click on formatting symbols or assign an AutoFormat. AutoFormats are report styles, which are suggested by the Wizard shortly before a report is finished. If you want to format an area differently, simply assign a new AutoFormat.

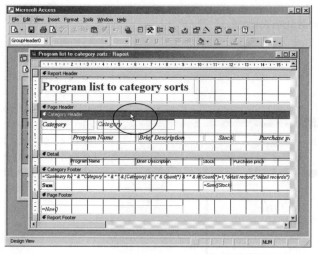

Mark the area you want to format by clicking on the area row.

Start the *AutoFormat* with this symbol.

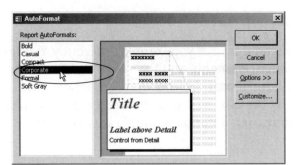

3 Again a list of the prepared report styles is displayed. Mark a suitable format.

4 There is also the possibility of leaving out attributes. For example, if you remove the tick next to Font, the AutoFormat will not change the font.

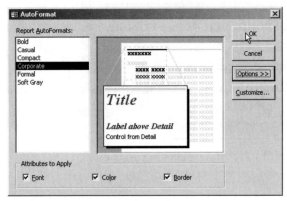

5 Assign the AutoFormat, ...

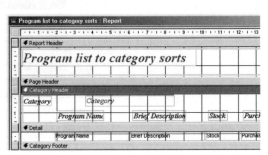

6 ... and your report area is automatically formatted in the new style.

Creating labels as reports

Although it is the most common report type, the single column report is not the only one that is used in practice. Often you have to print reports in table form or on prepared forms. Even to print labels you need a report. You will notice that Access not only knows the report type but also most label sizes.

Let's create a report, which prints labels with the names and divisions of members of staff. Create a query, which extracts first name and family name of staff members from the *Employees* table.

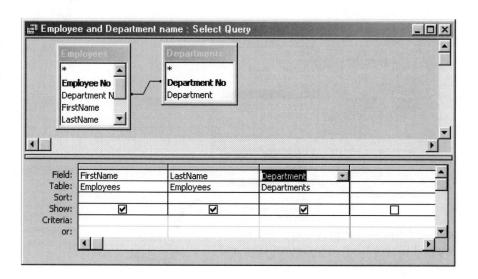

1 Start the next report in the Report module of the Database window.

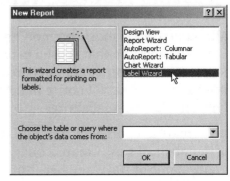

2 Switch to the Label Wizard, ...

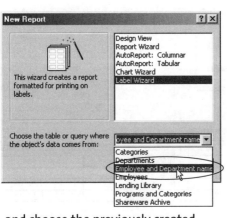

3 ... and choose the previously created query which contains members of staff and department names.

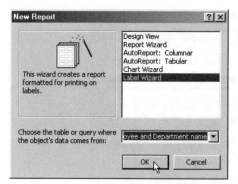

4 Proceed by clicking on the *OK* button.

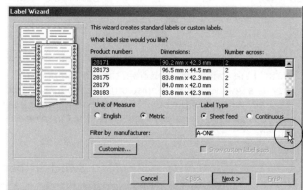

5 In the next window a list of computer label formats is displayed. First look for the manufacturer.

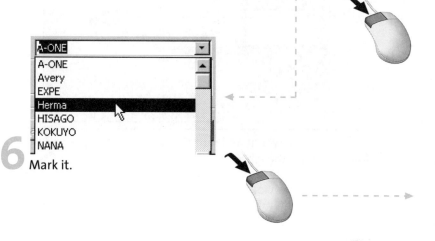

6 Mark it.

253

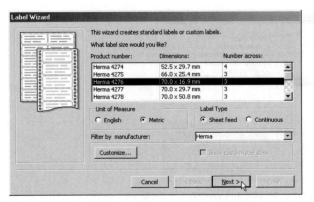

7 Then choose a suitable format from the list, and confirm your selection. The *Single* Label type contains a list of laser printer labels.

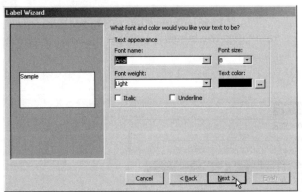

8 Now specify font and font size, as well as weight and font colour for the label.

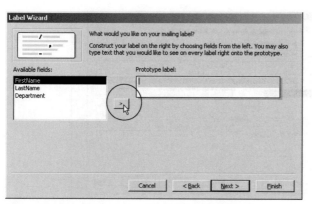

9 Then compile the fields from the query that you want to have on the label. Start with the first name.

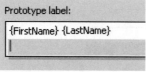

10 Press the Space bar once and then insert the family name into the label.

Prototype label:

{FirstName} {LastName}

11 Press the [↵] key to get into the next row.

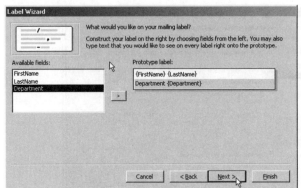

12 You can also enter text and only then adopt the field. Finish designing the label.

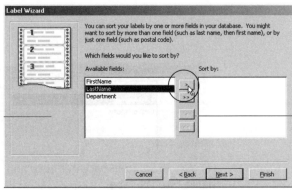

13 In the next step copy the field by which you want to sort into the right-hand column.

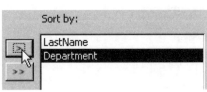

14 Insert the Department field as the second sorting field.

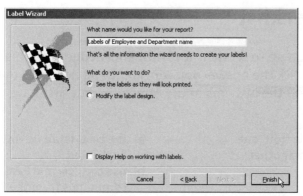

15 Enter a suitable name for the report. Then click on the *Finish* button.

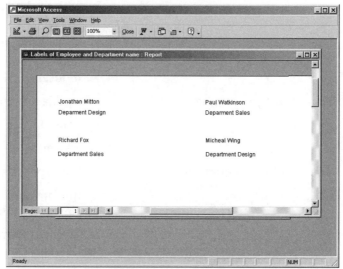

16 The result: individual data records are printed on the labels of the chosen format.

A brief checklist

Is your knowledge up to scratch? Test your knowledge with this exercise. Simply tick the answer you consider to be closest to the truth. You can find the answers in the Appendix (but first have a go!)

1. To copy a table from one database into another, ...

   a) the first database has to be deleted
   b) use the COPY and PASTE commands from the EDIT menu
   c) copy the table into an Excel window

2. Links can also be created in the relationship window ...

   a) the first database has to be deleted
   b) with the line tool from the toolbox
   c) by dragging the first field to the second with the mouse

3. For a report you require ...

   a) a table or a query
   b) at least three days
   c) a form

4. The report style determines ...

   a) the paper size of the report
   b) the font, font size, and line elements in the report
   c) who is authorised to access the report

5. As a rule the report title is entered in...

   a) the Detail area
   b) the Page Header
   c) without any reference to the report

6. Entire rows of elements ...

    a) cannot be marked

    b) do not exist

    c) can be marked with the mouse pointer at the left-hand row edge

7. The page number is usually entered ...

    a) as a formula in the Page Footer

    b) on a different sheet altogether

    c) as a formula in the Report Footer

8. You can view which fields have been included in the grouping under ...

    a) VIEW/FILTER

    b) VIEW/SORTING & GROUPING

    c) The detail records of the report

9. AutoFormat changes ...

    a) the style of a report

    b) the paper size of a report

    c) the settings in the table

10. The label size of the Label report ...

    a) cannot be modified

    b) can be chosen from many suggestions and be designed independently

    c) depends on the paper size of the report

You can find the answers to this brief checklist in the Appendix.

What's in this chapter:

In this chapter you are going to learn a few
advanced form techniques. For example,
you can significantly increase the efficiency
of your forms with
the help of sub-
forms. To revise,
you will create
tables, relational
links and queries
for the database.

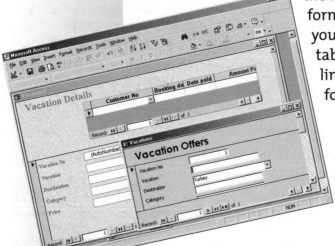

You already know about:

You are going to learn about:

The 'Vacations' Table module

You are the owner of a travel agency. As an advanced Access user you want to use your database program to manage the activities of your firm. These tasks are part of your work:

➔ Compiling a list of vacation offers

➔ Recording customer data

➔ Recording and analysing bookings

➔ Archiving completed bookings

The prerequisite for a functional database is again a database model with relational links between individual data collections. Start by creating a new database.

1 After the start-up of Access 2000 you can see the selection window. Choose the first option, ...

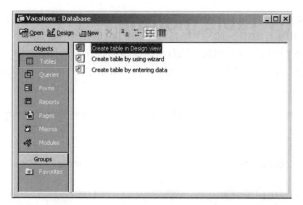

2 ... and enter the name of the new database: *Vacations*.
The MDB extension indicates that the file is an Access
database.

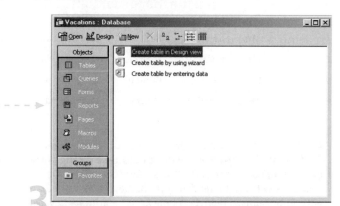

3 These are the tables you have to
create in the Table module. Start with
the *Customer* table.

Below follows an overview of the field structures of the individual
tables:

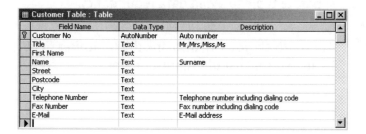

Field Name	Data Type	Description
Customer No	AutoNumber	Auto number
Title	Text	Mr,Mrs,Miss,Ms
First Name	Text	
Name	Text	Surname
Street	Text	
Postcode	Text	
City	Text	
Telephone Number	Text	Telephone number including dialing code
Fax Number	Text	Fax number including dialing code
E-Mail	Text	E-Mail address

The *Customer* table contains the data of the customers with complete address, phone number, and – for offers on the Internet – e-mail address. There is no place for data relating to booked or offered vacations in the customer table. You are going to create a separate table for these.

Immediately begin by entering the test data (fill in the remaining fields as you like):

Customer No	Title	First Name	Name	Street	Postcode	City
1	Mr	Paul	Dean	York Road	LS5 67CC	Leeds
2	Mrs	Margaret	Peters	Long Lane	S11 11KK	Sheffield
3	Mrs	Karen	Johnson	Orchard Grove	B12 13BB	Birmingham
4	Dr	Diane	Jones	Little Lane	SW10 1XX	London
5	Mrs	Valerie	Bird	London Road	Y90 90XX	York
6	Mr	Brian	Sawyers	Norwood Place	LS1 1CC	Leeds
7	Dr	Peter	Gilmore	Leeds Street	M13 0MM	Manchester
8	Mr	David	Melchett	Upton Road	OL5 5LL	Oldham

Now create the table with the vacation offers. It contains the vacation name from the catalogue, the price, and the travel dates. Create the *Destination* field as a Number field with the *Long Integer* size. The destinations are stored in a separate table to avoid data redundancy.

Alternatively you can also link the *Organiser* field to an external list of organiser names.

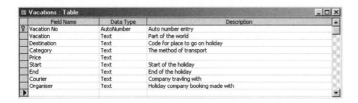

Here are a few test data for this table:

Vacation	Destination	Category	Price	Start	End	Courier	Organiser
Caribbean Dream	6	1	£ 770.00	01/06/98	14/06/98	Smith	Trash Tours
Majorca Experience	2	1	£ 300.00	12/05/98	19/05/98	Smith	Iberian Vacations
Greek Wine	4	1	£ 435.00	01/04/98	09/04/98	Murray	TUWI
Florence by Night	1	5	£ 135.00	14/03/98	21/03/98	Murray	TUWI

These are the two tables to which the Vacations list refers. Under *Category* the vacation types are stored, the field with the destinations contains the

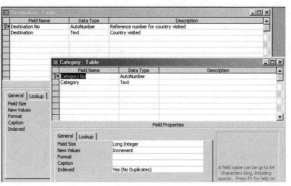

country names, and you could add further fields (airport, annotations, and so on).

Immediately enter the test data:

Category No	Category
1	Plane
2	Railway
3	Ship
4	Coach
5	Car

Destination No	Destination
1	Italy
2	Spain
3	Turkey
4	Greece
5	USA
6	Dominican Republic

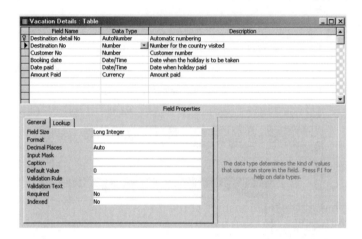

Finally the most important table: *Vacation Details*. Since you cannot save offers with any 'dynamic data' (bookings, completed bookings) in the table with the customer data or in the Vacations overview, you create a further table which is linked to these two data collections by means of linked fields. The table stores the bookings of the individual customers record by record. Apart from the booking date (important for cancellations) it also includes the date of payment, and a field for the amount actually paid. This amount will in practice differ from the price stored in the Vacation Offer, because of possible discounts, refunds, and so on.

Relationships

Create the relationships in the Relationship window by dragging a connecting line from the Primary Key field of one table to the linked field in the other table (as outlined in the previous chapter).

Activate the overview of the relationships of the individual tables with the TOOLS/RELATIONS menu command.

Insert all the tables by simply double-clicking on the table names.

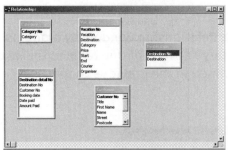

3 Arrange the individual field lists in the window. Then simply drag with the mouse pointer while pressing down the mouse button.

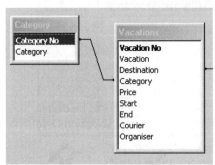

4 Draw in the first connecting line between the Vacations and Destinations tables.

5 Then insert a connection to the Category table.

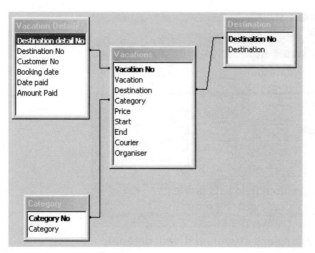

6 Finally, link the destination number in the Vacation Details table with the *Vacations* table.

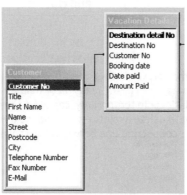

7 Now the only thing that remains to be done is to link the customer number to the *Vacation Details* table ...

269

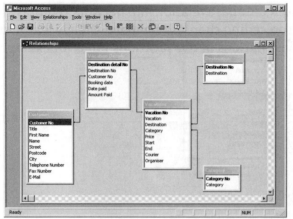

8... and the relationships in your relational database are perfect.

9 Save the layout and close it.

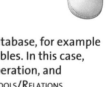

Creating forms

You can create forms for data entry in the individual tables. For this purpose, mark the table name in the Table module and activate the function on the toolbar. AutoForms are created without any further need for confirmation. You only need to save them under a form name.

However, our complex database relationship network requires easier entry masks. In the preceding chapters you have already learnt how to offer the list of destinations in the Vacations table, for example:

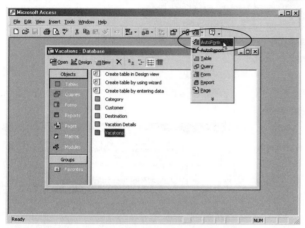

1 Start with AutoForm for the Vacations table.

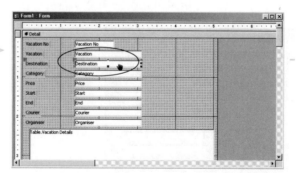

2 Immediately switch into Design View and delete the Destination field which after all only contains the destination number.

271

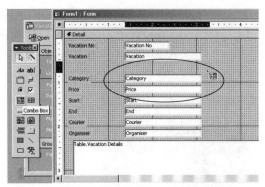

3 Draw in a new field with the Combination Field tool.

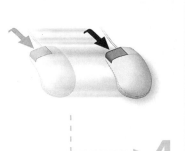

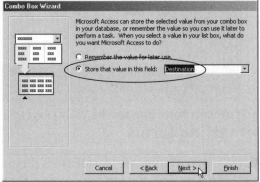

4 Answer the questions of the Wizard, insert the destination name into the field, and link it to the field in the Vacations list.

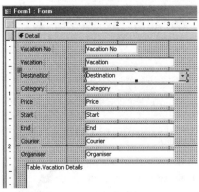

5 The combination field is complete. In the same way create the field for the vacation category.

You can activate the **Toolbox** by means of the toolbar if it is not displayed.

If the Wizard does not start for the production of a combination field, activate it in the Toolbox, too.

Formatting forms

However useful they are, AutoForms do not look nice. Familiarise yourself with a few design techniques for forms:

☞ Drag the bottom right-hand corner of the form area to enlarge the form.

☞ Open a new area for the title with the VIEW/FORM HEADER/FOOTER menu command. Draw in a Label element and enter the *Vacation Offers* title.

☞ Mark all Label fields in the left-hand part of the form and choose the FORMAT/ALIGN/RIGHT menu command.

☞ Drag the marking frame across all Label and Text fields and choose the FORMAT/VERTICAL DISTANCE/ENLARGE menu command twice.

Ctrl+A also selects all the elements in the form.

The 'Bookings' form

Bookings for individual vacations are entered into the Vacation Details table, since you have designated the customer number and the vacation number as a relationship field. Now you could create a form for this table, delete the elements designated for the Number fields and create combination fields for the Customer and Vacations lists.

However, there is an alternative method: change the structure of the table so that it already 'knows' where the customer data and the vacation offers come from. When you now create a form from the table, it automatically has the suitable combination fields.

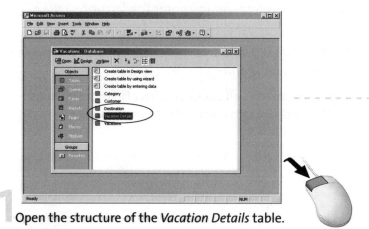

Open the structure of the *Vacation Details* table.

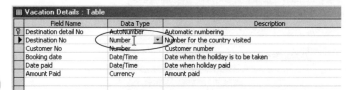

2 Mark the linked Number field with the *Vacation No*, ...

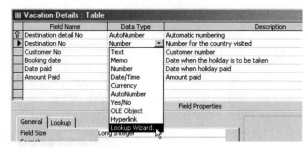

3 ... and choose the Wizard drop-down list from the Data Type list.

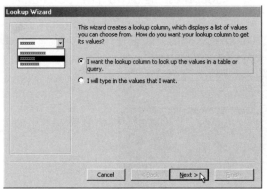

4 Confirm the first step as it is.

5 *Vacations* is the table which provides the data to the field.

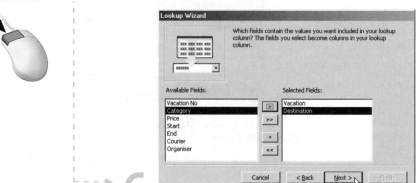

6 Adopt these fields from the other table.

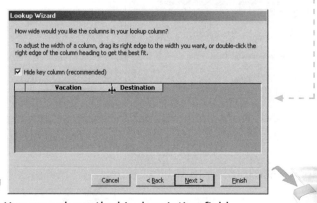

7 You can enlarge the big description field by dragging.

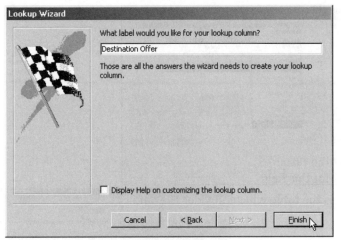

8 Now enter the new column heading for the field, ...

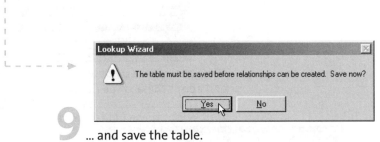

9 ... and save the table.

With these operations you have prepared the table so that, instead of the number, the two fields from the *Vacations* table are automatically integrated, that is, in forms and in data sheets. The same procedure is now also required for the field containing the customer number, since this originates from a different table:

277

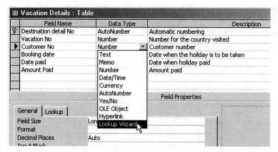

1 Again start the Wizard drop-down list for this field.

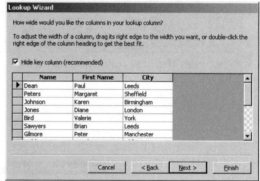

2 Specify the *Customer* table as data supplier, and adopt these three fields.

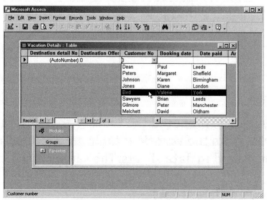

3 Confirm the remaining steps. Save and close the structure of the table. You can already operate the two drop-down lists in Data Sheet View.

Subsequently you can create an AutoForm for this table. It will not only create the links to the *Vacation Details* table but also those to the *Customer* and *Vacations* linked tables.

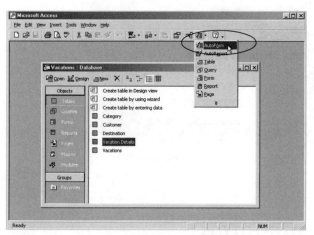

The queries must be marked in the Objects module. Start AutoForm with the symbol on the toolbar.

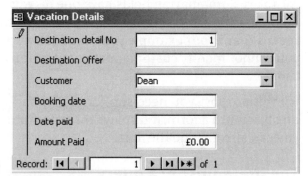

That's it! You have a fully functional form for the bookings. The combination fields such as the *Customer* field ...

3 ... automatically integrate the data recorded in the other tables.

Forms and sub-forms

The option to work in a form with combination fields, which offer data from other linked tables, makes the database very flexible. Furthermore, if you rely on the Wizard, you cannot make a lot of mistakes. Combination fields have one disadvantage: you cannot enter new data and save it back to your basis tables. In practice this means that in our example you may book vacations with a form, but you cannot modify customer data or vacation offers at the same time.

For this purpose you need sub-forms. The sub-form is integrated as an object into a form. It displays the data from another table, and in it you can also change the data.

The prerequisite: a query

You have to create a query, which integrates data for forms based on several data collections. Create such a form for the *Vacation Offers* and *Vacation Details* tables:

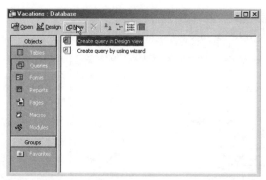

1 In the Query module of the Database
window click on the *New* button.

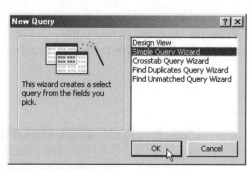

2 A Wizard is going to help you.

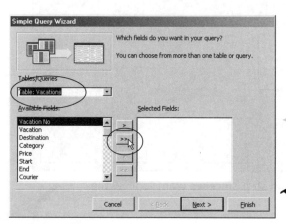

3 Begin with the *Vacations* table. Adopt all the
fields from the table.

281

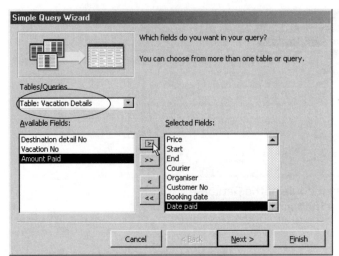

4 From the *Vacation Details* table you need the fields
Customer No, *Booking date*, *Date paid*, and *Amount Paid*.

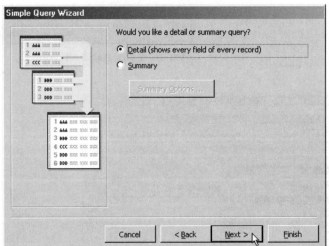

5 Confirm the next step, since we want to view the
Details, ...

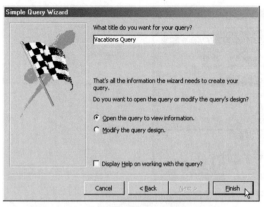

6 ... and save the query under this name.

Subsequently you can again view the query in the Query Design. Then close the window.

The sub-form

You only have to enter the customer data separately. This could also be done by means of the sub-form (but that would be taking things too far).

To record the bookings we will now create a combination of form and sub-form. This form will offer you the option to simultaneously record new vacation offers and their booking dates.

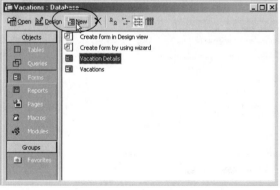

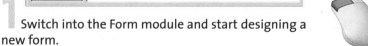

1 Switch into the Form module and start designing a new form.

Again the Form Wizard will assist you. From the list below choose the recently created query 'Vacations and Vacation Details'.

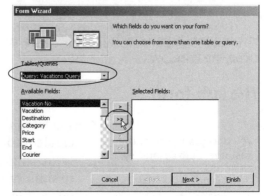

You have already carefully selected the list in the query, therefore you can adopt the entire list.

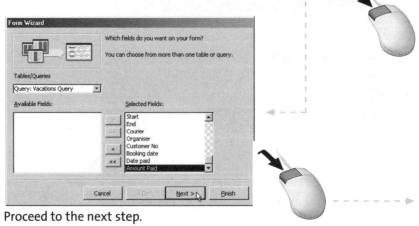

Proceed to the next step.

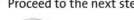

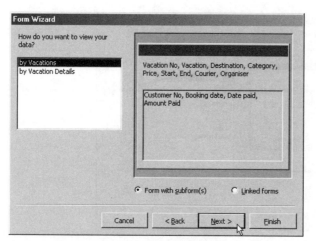

5 Here you determine the division between main
form and sub-form. In this case the data is displayed
by vacations, thus the vacation offers are the main form.

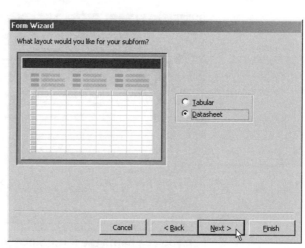

6 In the next step you determine the
layout for the sub-form. The Data Sheet
View is optimal but you could also view
the table.

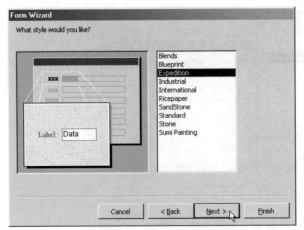

7 Now choose a style, which determines the background, font, and font size.

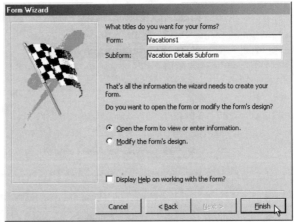

8 Then you can name the form. Since you have to save a sub-form at the same time, you need to enter a name for it, too.

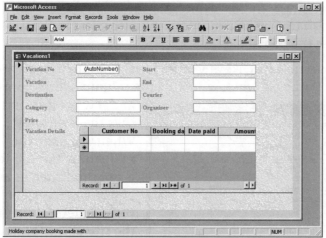

 9 This is the result: the main form offers the vacation offers from the *Vacations* table; in the sub-form you can enter the bookings which are then saved in *Vacation Details*.

> The Wizard has already offered a different combination, namely two linked forms. This is an alternative to the sub-form technique. Simply place the two forms next to each other and edit them at the same time.

If you cannot see the sub-form as data sheet, open the Design and change the view in the Properties window of the sub-form element.

Please note the two navigation buttons at the bottom of the form:

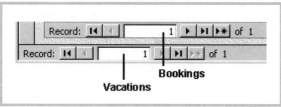

the arrows inside refer to the sub-form, and the navigation buttons for the data records of the main form are at the edge.

287

Now record the data with this form: enter the bookings for the already existing vacation offers, choose the customers in the sub-form, and enter the booking dates.

You can edit the sub-form like any other form. Activate it in the Form module of the Database window, modify the column widths, fonts,

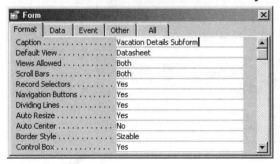

and row heights, and save the form again. When you open the main form, the sub-form is only indicated as an object. However, here you can determine the size of the form.

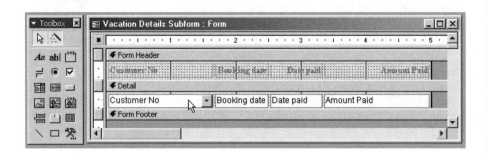

A brief checklist

Enter the correct expressions in the gaps.

The fields in a table structure which are linked to fields in other tables must have the _____ (1) field data type. The sizes of these fields are specified with _____ (2). Relationships between the tables can be viewed and modified under _____ (3) Tools. To create a relationship the _____ (4) of the first table is dragged onto the linked field of the other table. With the _____ (5) key you can delete a selected Relationship line. You can right-align form elements with the _____ (6) menu. Increase the vertical distance with the _____ (7) option from this menu. A sub-form offers the data from a _____ (8) table or query for editing. When a sub-form is located in a main form you can see _____ (9) different navigation buttons. The outside arrows control the data records in the _____ (10).

You can find the answers to this brief checklist in the Appendix.

9

What's in this chapter?

If up to now you have used a text-processing
program to write your invoices, you will not
have automated very much in your data
collections. It is not possible to integrate more
than one address list into the Mail Merge
function. This chapter
will show you the
possibilities Access
offers for such tasks.
You will also be shown
how to convert Access
data into Excel tables
or make them
available to Word.
Furthermore, you
can familiarise
yourself with data
protection.

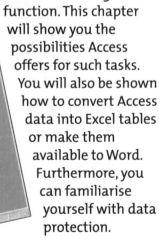

Handling orders

Everybody who is working with invoicing programs or who has done so in the past is familiar with this problem. Writing an invoice does not simply mean taking a sheet of paper; writing the address of the customer on it; then listing the individual items; and finally entering the total plus VAT at the bottom after having calculated it with a calculator.

If you want to work in a reasonably organised fashion, you will create an order system that also automatically writes your invoices with Access. The invoice automatically depends on the data records in the Order table, which is linked to the customer and product data.

In the preceding chapters you had ample opportunity to train in creating links and relational relationships. In all these case Access provides helpful Wizards to assist you.

Now you are going to meet a Wizard which creates an entire database for handling orders and which also provides an automatic invoice-creation process. You can easily modify this database to suit your requirements.

Creating the database

1 After the start-up of Access you are presented with an overview of the databases you have edited up to now. Choose the second option with the Database Wizard.

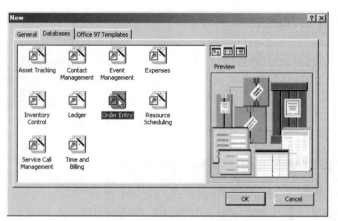

Here you can find all the Wizards. The Wizard we are looking for is called *Order Entry*. Select it, ...

... and start by clicking on OK.

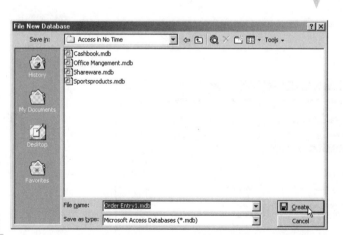

The Wizard suggests a name for the database. Adopt it, ...

File name: Order Entry

5 ... or enter a name of your choice, ...

... and confirm it. **6**

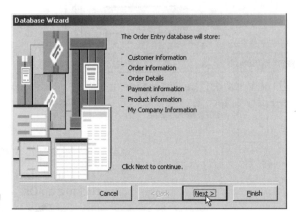

Database Wizard

The Order Entry database will store:

- Customer information
- Order information
- Order Details
- Payment information
- Product information
- My Company Information

Click Next to continue.

Cancel   < Back   Next >   Finish

7 This message tells you what
the Wizard is going to create.

Confirm this
dialog box, too. **8**

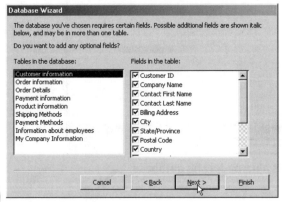

Database Wizard

The database you've chosen requires certain fields. Possible additional fields are shown italic
below, and may be in more than one table.

Do you want to add any optional fields?

Tables in the database:	Fields in the table:
Customer information	☑ Customer ID
Order information	☑ Company Name
Order Details	☑ Contact First Name
Payment information	☑ Contact Last Name
Product information	☑ Billing Address
Shipping Methods	☑ City
Payment Methods	☑ State/Province
Information about employees	☑ Postal Code
My Company Information	☑ Country

Cancel   < Back   Next >   Finish

9 The Wizard now offers you the tables with
field lists.

Please note that some of the fields serve as Primary Key fields for the links. It is best to leave all the fields in the tables. You can always delete them later on in Table Design.

These field lists are of course only suggestions. You do not have to adopt any. Simply remove the ticks in front of the fields from those you do not need in your database. You can click on the fields in Italics to integrate them into your table, too.

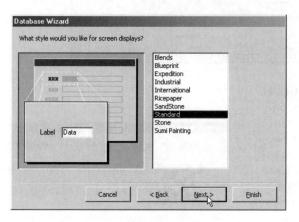

10 In the next step the Wizard asks you which style you want to apply to your screens. This refers to the backgrounds, the fonts, and the font sizes in the forms. Keep them simple, since excessive formatting only gets in the way when you edit the form elements.

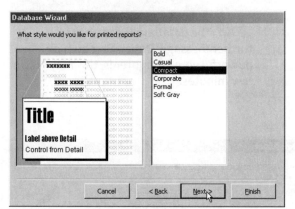

11 The same applies to reports: if kept simple and compact, they do not take up too much space and are easier to edit.

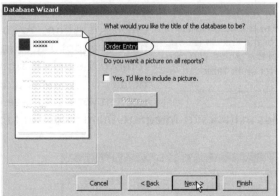

12 With this you have worked through all the steps. Now you only have to tell the Wizard the name of your new database (this refers to forms and reports, since you have entered the name of the database before).

13 The database is set up after a further message. Depending on how powerful your computer is, this may take a few minutes.

14 Finally, you are prompted to enter the basic data of your company.

My Company Information ☒

Enter your company's name and address information here. You will save the information by closing the form.

Company MCT   Default Terms
Address   Invoice Descr
City   Phone Number
State/Province   Fax Number
Postal Code
Country
Sales Tax Rate 0.00%

15 Enter your data into the form and then close it.

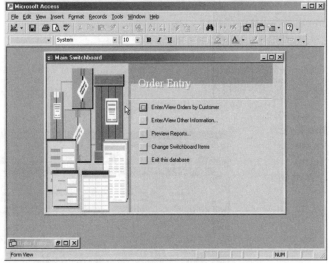

16 Subsequently the Start form is displayed. The Database window is reduced to icon size and placed at the bottom left.

To jolt your memory: this Main Overview, which is nothing more than a form, is set as the Start form under the TOOLS/START menu command.

Relationships

Relationships are the most important part of the relational database. The Wizard has done everything in its power to create a complex, functional network of tables and to link these. If you have diligently worked through the preceding chapters you will not find it difficult to unravel this web:

1 Choose the TOOLS/ RELATIONS menu command.

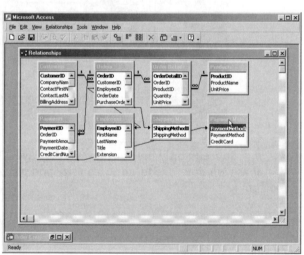

2 The Relationship window is displayed. Drag one table with the mouse pointer in the Title bar, ...

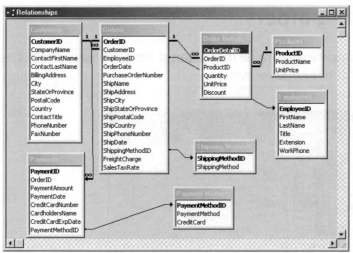

3 ... and arrange the individual lists so that the relationships become visible.

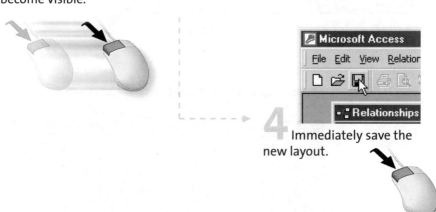

4 Immediately save the new layout.

Incidentally, you can already recognise by the line which links two tables what kind of relationship you are dealing with. If the line becomes thicker at its ends, it is a relationship with referential integrity, that is, this relationship prevents the deleting of data that are still connected to other tables. The relationships also display the relationship type (standard 1:n). The 1 represents a field which may exist once, whereas the 'infinity' sign represents n data records (for example, a distinct customer number in the Customer table, which however may appear n-times in the Orders table).

299

Entering orders

Orders are entered on a form you can simply call up with the first option of the Main Overview.

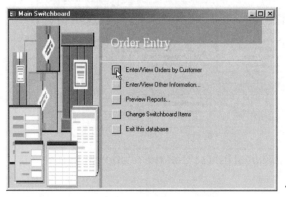

On the Start form click on the first option.

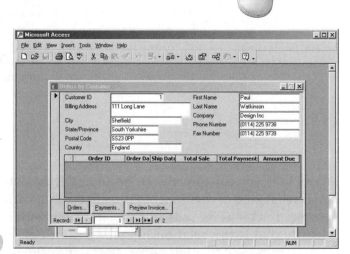

The form opens. Enter a few data records. Switch from one field to the next by pressing the Enter key.

3

| Record: |◄| ◄| | 1 |►| ►|| ►* | of 2 |

You can scroll from record to record with the Data Record Navigator. The Star symbol deletes the mask for the next new data record.

4 Click on the *Orders* button.

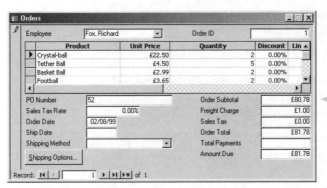

5 Then open the sub-form in which you can deal with individual orders. Enter further records for the customer shown, or edit already recorded orders.

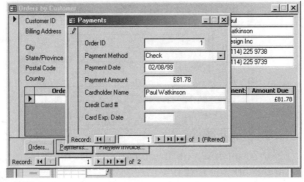

6 The *Payments* button takes you to another linked form, in which the customer's payment conditions are listed.

How do you create such buttons? Drawing the objects is easy. However, to link them with the table data you need to use module programming. Buttons start modules. Modules are programs written in Visual Basic. They are stored in the Module module of the Database window. Find out which module is behind a button:

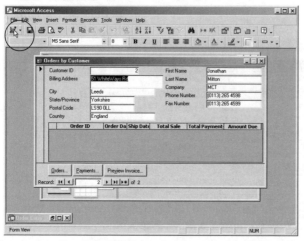

1 As soon as the Order form is displayed, switch into Design View.

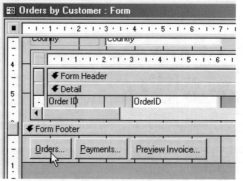

2 Scroll down until you can see the buttons, and mark the first one.

3 Open the Properties window with this symbol (or by double-clicking on the button).

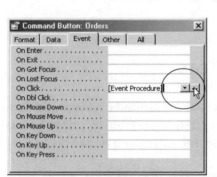

4 On the *Event* tab you can find the event properties. Our button starts, *when clicked*, a procedure which you can view.

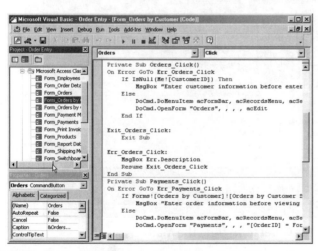

5 The Visual Basic Editor window shows the VBA module with the button procedure, which is started when the button is clicked.

303

We are not going to deal in any more depth with the buttons, since it
would go beyond the scope of this book.

Creating invoices

The writing of invoices is also planned on the main form, even if there
is no separate option for it. It is possible to print the invoice
immediately after recording or editing data and again at the touch of
a button.

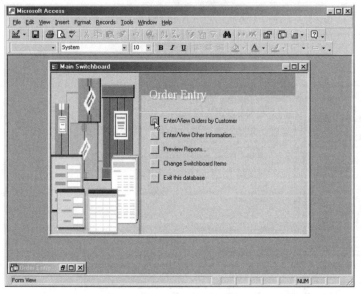

Again start the Order form from the Main
Overview.

2 Scroll to the data record of
the customer whom you want
to invoice, and click on the
Preview Invoice button.

3 Here you can enter or modify a few
basic invoice data. When you click on the
OK button ...

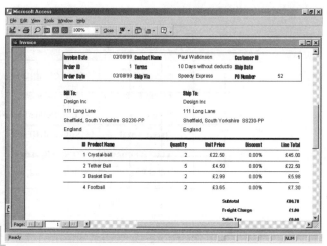

4 ... the invoice is printed out as a report.

305

5 Have a look at the Report Design.

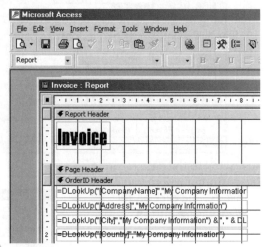

6 Grouping has been carried out by order numbers. The address details are entered into the grouping area.

7 The actual invoice data can be found in the Detail area, ...

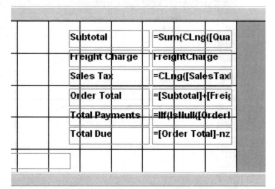

8 ... and the Footer area contains the totals, and the tax and invoice amounts.

TIP

By pressing ⇧+F2, your formula is displayed in a zoom window.

A closer examination of the individual formulas is useful. Open the Properties window of any element and study the calculations. You can find them as control element contents on the last tab called *All*.

Exporting data to Excel

The spreadsheet program Excel is one of the particularly useful elements of the Office package. It is often not easy for users to decide whether Excel or Access is the best tool for their work. However, Excel is usually the easier option if you need quick results.

However, there is a simple way of distinguishing between the two: Excel does not support relational links. As soon as you are dealing with different data collections (customers and orders, products and suppliers, and so on), you should use Access.

You can export the data from your Access database into an Excel table to calculate the Number fields with formulas and functions, as this is something which Access cannot do quite as well. For example, this is how to edit the total of sales in Excel in order to create a chart:

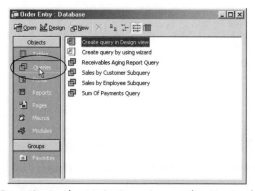

1 Deactivate the Main Overview and activate the Database window.

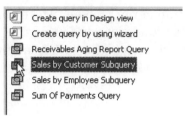

Mark this query, ...

Merge It with MS Word
Publish It with MS Word
Analyze It with MS Excel

3 ... and copy the query result into an Excel table.

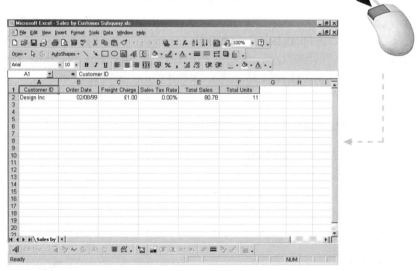

4 The table immediately opens in the Excel window. You can now start with your calculations or the creation of a chart.

If Excel is not active as a program, it is automatically opened with this data export. The workbook that is created can be stored as an XLS file on your hard disk.

TIP

You can transfer tables as well as queries to Excel. With the FILE/SAVE AS/EXPORT menu command you can also export data to Excel or any other data format.

Experienced Excel users also know the reverse way, namely data import. From Excel you can also move Access data into an Excel table. The special advantage of this method: you can dynamically link data, that is, import data in such a way that each change in the Access database is automatically reflected in the Excel table.

Data import is carried out with the DATA/GET EXTERNAL DATA/NEW DATABASE QUERY menu commands. Queries are edited with MS Query, which is very similar to the Access Query module.

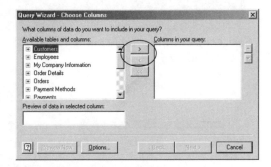

Creating a Word Mail Merge file

The text processing program Word offers a Mail Merge function with which you can send a text document to several addressees. Whether you send publicity brochures to customers, distribute information to colleagues, or get quotes from several companies, in each of these cases the data source should be an Access database. Access data can be maintained and updated, which is not as easy in Word tables.

An example from practice: you wish to use the *Customer* table from our Orders database as the data source for a PR brochure for your company. This is how you can create a form letter with variable customer data:

Select the *Customer* table in the Table module of the Database window.

Merge It with MS Word
Publish It with MS Word
Analyze It with MS Excel

This is where you start to export data into a form letter.

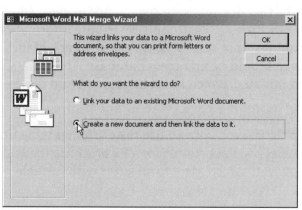

Microsoft Word Mail Merge Wizard

This wizard links your data to a Microsoft Word document, so that you can print form letters or address envelopes.

OK

Cancel

What do you want the wizard to do?

○ Link your data to an existing Microsoft Word document.

○ Create a new document and then link the data to it.

If you do not already have a suitable document, it will now be created.

4 Word starts. The new form letter with the Mail Merge toolbar has already been prepared. Insert the fields from the *Customer* table.

5 Start with the *Company* field, ...

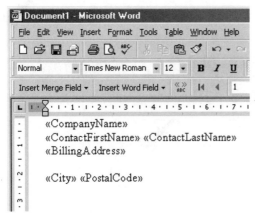

6 ... and one by one insert all address fields. Press the ⏎ key to get to a new line and do not forget the spaces between the fields.

311

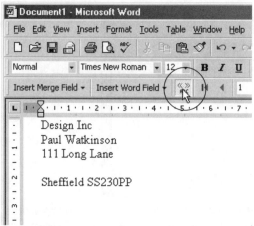

7 With this symbol you can check the data records in a preview.

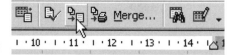

8 Here you can start printing the form letter into a document, ...

9 ... or with this symbol on the connected printer.

With the TOOLS/MAIL MERGE menu command you can control and correct the link to the Access data source if necessary.

Protecting databases with database passwords

The password which you enter at the start-up of the operating system is a generally secure protection from unauthorised access, at least if you work under Windows NT. Windows 95 and 98 do not protect data. If you create and maintain Access databases which contain data that must not be accessed by anybody else using your PC, you should protect the databases separately. Simply assign a password ...

CAUTION

... which you must not forget. There is no official way to reproduce a forgotten password. If you cannot remember your password, you will not be able to access your data.

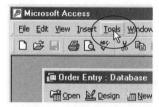

1 To assign a password, activate the TOOLS menu ...

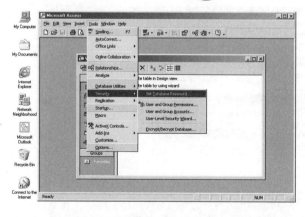

2 ... and the first menu option under SECURITY.

3 Enter the password. Confirm it with the second entry. Both entries are only displayed as asterisks.

4 When you close the database and immediately open it again, you are asked for the password.

The password can consist of up to 20 characters. Passwords are case-sensitive. You can delete an existing password under the same menu option.

You can find further security measures under the TOOLS/SECURITY menu command. When you activate the User Level Security Wizard, it securely leads you to a secure database.

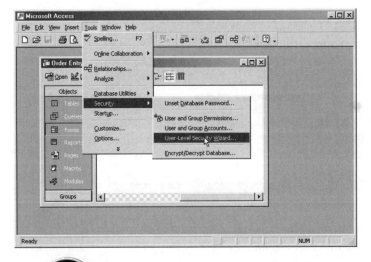

A brief checklist

Now test your knowledge for the last time. Answer the ten questions with *Right* or *Wrong*, and only then check whether you were right.

Question	Right	Wrong
1. There is a separate Database Wizard for orders.		
2. You cannot manually edit the Start form.		
3. A thicker connecting line in the Relationship window indicates referential integrity.		
4. Buttons in forms usually activate a VBA module (procedure).		
5. The Order Wizard produces invoices on forms.		
6. In the grouping part of the report the data of the recipient of the invoice are stored.		
7. Access should be chosen instead of Excel if tables have to be linked.		
8. An Access table cannot be used as a data source for Word form letters.		
9. There is no limit to the length of a database password.		
10. The User Data Security Wizard offers comprehensive database protection.		

You will find the answers in the appendix.

What's in this chapter?

This is something that will keep happening to you: your program simply refuses to do what you want it to do, reacting only with an incomprehensible error message. Alternatively, it will fill your screen with something you do not know and cannot classify. What can you do?

The most important rule first: everything has a reason. The program will not do anything (almost) which does not have an explainable and reparable cause. Therefore you should first try to narrow it down to possible errors. Use the Access Help functions, carefully read the Help text, and try again.

In this chapter you can find some of these 'unexplainable phenomena' and insoluble tasks as well as the corresponding solutions.

Where can I get help quickly?

The Office Assistant

Your lively little friend will stand by with moral and practical support. It often offers its help without being asked, but you can deactivate and activate it when you need it at any time.

1 Open the Help menu, and choose the first MICROSOFT ACCESS HELP option to activate the Assistant (or click on the yellow symbol with the question mark in a speech balloon).

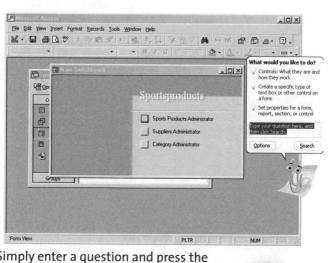

2 Simply enter a question and press the ⏎ key. The Assistant immediately offers all the available Help texts.

What would you like to do?

💡 Restrict or validate data

💡 Define or view relationships

💡 Add or manipulate fields
(Microsoft Access)

💡 Define or change a primary
key

💡 Define or change data types

See more...

Type your question here, and
then click Search.

| Options | Search |

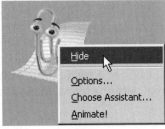

3 You can activate the offered Help items by simply clicking on the yellow symbol.

TIP
Alternatively you can press the F1 key to activate the Assistant.

Hide
Options...
Choose Assistant...
Animate!

4 When you click on the Question mark icon again, the Help is deactivated. You can switch off the Assistant in the context menu which opens when you right-click on it.

Context help and help window

You can call up the Access Help menu at any time and read through the long list of explanations. Furthermore, you can use the alphabetical keyword index in which you can also search for Help topics.

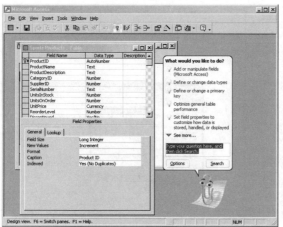

1 Activate the Help with the F1 key or by clicking on the Question Mark icon. The Assistant will offer you Help texts which relate to your work (Context Help, here relating to Field Properties).

2 If you cannot find a suitable Help text, simply enter a keyword.

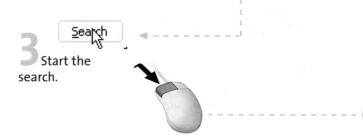

3 Start the search.

 The Help window opens. You get help relating to the searched-for expression. Activate one of the Help texts shown.

Read through the Help text and use the buttons offered. To get a complete overview of all topics activate the tabs.

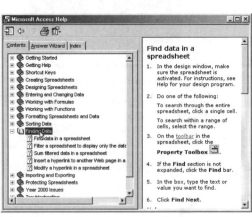

Here you can surely find what you are looking for. Also use the *Contents* and *Index* tabs.

What's this? or ScreenTips

You do not understand a menu command? You cannot make out what an icon is for? Then you can use *What's This?*, which gives you information on what you click on:

1 From the Help menu choose What's This? or press the ⇧+F1 keyboard shortcut.

2 Activate a menu item or click on the icon you want to have explained.

Startup (Tools menu)

Controls and customizes various database startup properties and actions, such as application title and icon, and which startup form or data access page to display.

3 A small ScreenTips window opens displaying a description of the selected menu item.

The operation (for example, *Save, Open, and Print*) which is called up by the menu item or symbol is not executed in this case.

The Help dialog

There is yet another Help and it is – although difficult to spot – particularly useful when dealing with dialog boxes. When you open a dialog field you can call up a small Help text for many individually displayed options in the active dialog box. Example:

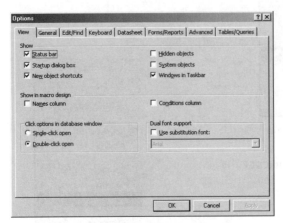

1 Activate the Options dialog box with the TOOLS/ OPTIONS menu command.

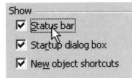

2 Place the mouse pointer on the first option on the *View* tab, then press the right mouse button.

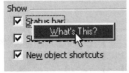

3 Now you can call up a brief Help text for this option.

Select **Status Bar** to display the status bar at the bottom of the Microsoft Access window.

4 Read the *What's This?* text and close the dialog box again.

Help, I cannot find my database!

There may be several reasons why you cannot open your database after the start-up of Access. Usually the database file has (accidentally) been deleted, moved, or renamed. Try to locate the file on your hard disk. Let's assume you are looking for the *Customer Management.mdb* database:

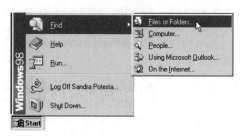

From the Start menu choose the FIND command and in the submenu the FILES/ FOLDERS command.

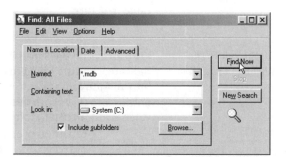

Enter the name into the entry box. Part of the filename will be enough. If you want to look for all databases enter *.mdb. Start the search by clicking on the *Find Now* button.

Now the entire hard disk is searched for the file or files. The locations are then displayed in the Results window. Have a look at the second column. It will tell you in which folder your database is located.

Help, my table has packed up!

When you are working with tables in the Table Design or in Table View all sorts of problems will crop up every now and again. Below you can find a list of such problems and the corresponding solutions:

Problem	Solution
The column is not wide enough to accommodate the data.	You can increase the column width of every column by dragging the right-hand line of the column to the right in the column heading.
I can only enter a limited number of characters.	In this case the field length is probably not large enough. Switch to the table Design View and change the first option in the field properties (field size) for this field.
The column should have a different name.	Easy. Simply choose the FORMAT/RENAME COLUMN menu command. Enter a new column name. This is then also the new field name in the table structure.
I cannot enter anything into the column. I can only hear a sound signal.	Keep an eye on the Status bar, which will also indicate if you are trying to make an entry into an AutoValue field. You cannot make entries into fields with this data type; the value is automatically calculated.
The entry into a field is not adopted. How can I get out of this again?	When you have made a wrong entry (for example, text into a Number field) the data record is nevertheless marked as 'modified'. Press the (Esc) key to leave the field.
I want to restore a deleted data record but the UNDO option in the EDIT menu is not active.	This option is rarely active when you are editing or entering data, since all changes are automatically saved in the database. This also means that deleted data records are lost for good.

Problem	Solution
I always have to enter phone numbers in a particular format, so that the entry is accepted. How can I avoid this?	Switch to the Design View of the table. When you place the cursor in the field with the phone number, you can see below in the field properties under *Entry Format* an entry mask, which you can delete at any time.
A field in my table contains a list of suggestions. I want to enter my own contents but I cannot.	The field has been created with the Drop-Down List Wizard and it presumably gets the data from another table. Open the table in Design View and re-activate the Wizard. It also offers an option that permits you to enter your own data.

Help, my form does not do what I want it to do!

Forms are the most efficient tools for data entry but only as long as they work properly. A faulty form can cost you a lot of time and mental energy. You may avoid this by reading this information about the Form View:

Problem	Solution
When I press the ⏎ key in a particular field the marking jumps to the wrong field.	The activation order is not correct. Switch into the Design View of the form, and choose the VIEW/ACTIVATION ORDER menu command. Place the mouse pointer in the grey box at the left-hand edge, and drag the field that is in the wrong place into the correct position.
My form is much longer than it should be. This has the disadvantage that I cannot see all its fields at once, whereas there is a big gap at the bottom.	This is the Form Footer. Hide this area which usually you will not need. Open the form in Design View, and drag the bottom line of the form upwards until the *Form Footer* area is closed.

Problem	Solution
My form contains fields on a second page, although there is still enough space on the first page. How can I avoid the laborious scrolling?	You have to arrange the fields correspondingly in the Form Design. Also check that you have not inserted a page break. This is a small dotted line at the left-hand edge of the Design window.
A form from my Form module does not show any data. What has happened?	Check to which table the form is linked. Switch into Design View and double-click on the small black square in the top left-hand corner in which the two rulers meet. Check the data origin in the Properties window. If the table or query displayed here does not contain any data, the form will also be empty.
I cannot label the first field with the *AutoValue* data type anyway. How can I lock this form element so that it will not be selected at all?	Select the control element in Design View, and open the Properties window. On the second tab (*Data*) you can find the *Activated Locked* properties. Set the first to *No* and the second to *Yes*.
Date values are always displayed in the shortest format. Is it possible to extend the display so that, for example, the month is written out in full?	It is, namely in Design View again. Open the properties of the control element and mark the *Entry Format* row. When you click on the icon to the right of the row a Wizard appears which helps you to apply an extended date format.
When I create a combination field, the Wizard no longer appears. What has happened?	You have accidentally deactivated the icon on the top right of the Toolbox. This is where the Wizard is activated.

Help, my query does not work!

The query as the basis for forms or reports sums up data from different tables. Pay particular attention to the correct relationships, and do not use fields that do not exist.

Problem	Solution
Two tables with 20 data records each are involved in my query. When I carry out the query I get 400 records as result. What is wrong with the query?	The two tables are not linked. If there is more than one table in the Query window, a connecting line must point from the Primary Key field of the one to a Number field of the other.
I have forgotten to insert a table at the start. Can I insert it now?	Choose the QUERY/SHOW TABLE menu command. Now you can insert further Table windows. If you do not need a window any more, delete it with the Del key.
My query does not show some of the fields, although they are listed in the Query window.	Check whether there is a tick in the *Show* row of the respective fields.
I am trying to sort the query result by several fields. By which field is it sorted first?	The field which is furthest to the left in the Query Design.
How can I sort the query by a field that is not shown?	Drag the field name to the left into the first column, and remove the tick in the *Show* row.
I want to write the result of a query in a new table. How do I proceed?	In the *Query* menu choose the *Create Table Query* command. It creates a new table.
When I start my query a dialog box requesting a field I do not recognise is displayed. What has gone wrong?	You have used a field name in a column that does not exist (any more). Perhaps you have deleted the field in the table structure, or it maybe a simple typing mistake.

Problem	Solution
What has gone wrong if the query result is always empty ?	Usually it means that the criteria in the Criteria row are wrong. Narrow down the problem by taking each field separately into the query, entering criteria, and running the query.

Help, my report does not show what I want it to show!

The Report Design is even more complex than the Form Design. The numerous areas are not easy to manage. It will take some time until you produce the first really useful reports.

Problem	Solution
My report shows all the labels but it does not show any data records.	Check the data origin. If you click in Report Design at the top left on the box with the small black square, you can read in the Properties field which table or query is feeding the data.
The line spacing in my report is much too big.	Open the Report Design and examine the Detail area. If you drag the top line of the following area very close to the control elements, the spacing will be reduced. You may have to select the elements with a mouse click on their left and move them to the very top.
How can I delete a grouping element I do not need any more?	After calling up the VIEW/SORTING & GROUPING menu command all the grouping fields are shown. Select the row containing the field and choose *No* under *Grouping Header*. This removes the grouping from the report.

Problem	Solution
My report does not fit onto one page in Portrait format.What can I do? Do I have to reduce all the control panel elements one by one?	No, you don't. First try to sort out the problem by reducing the page margins or adjusting the column widths under FILE/PAGE SETUP.
If I want to reduce a report column, I first have to edit the label in the Page Header and then the element in the Detail area. Isn't there a quicker way?	Yes, there is. Simply draw a frame around both elements with the mouse to select them. If you now reduce one element, it will also affect the other.
How can I print data on a form that already has a pre-printed Print Report Header and Footer?	Choose the FILE/PAGE SETUP menu command. On the first tab (margins) you can find the *Data Only* option.

Checklist answers

In this Appendix you will find the answers to the checklists in the individual chapters.

Chapter 1

The acronym DBMS stands for **Database Management System** (1). It refers to the software with which a database is managed.

Databases consist of **tables** (2), forms, **queries** (3), reports, macros, and modules.

The core of a database is formed by tables, which are linked to each other. A database with links is called **relational** (4).

In a table every column is referred to as **field** (5). The column heading is also the field name. To pre-define the column heading or contents its **field property** (6) must be modified.

Access 2000 can be started either with the **Start menu** (7) or the Shortcut bar.

An Access 2000 database is saved in a file with the **MDB** extension (8). The file can have a size of up to 1 **gigabyte** (9).

The default database folder is defined with the **Tools/Options** menu command (10).

The tables in the *Northwind.mdb* example database are linked. The links can be viewed with the **Tools/Relationships** menu command (11).

The Database window contains six (12) modules. With the **Design** button (13) an object (for example, a table) can be viewed in Design View. To the left on the toolbar you will find an icon with which you can immediately switch the table into **Data Sheet View** (14).

Chapter 2

1. No, of course not. You can create as many tables as you like. Only the size of your memory limits this number.

2. This is correct. MDB stands for *Microsoft DataBase*.

3. No, up to 64 characters are permitted, and thus also numbers and a few special characters.

4. The field data types are restricted to the ten that are available in the Table Design.

5. No, the primary key is attached to the field that is distinct in the table.

6. No, only if the marking is in the last field of a row. Otherwise the ⏎ key takes you to the next field.

7. This is correct, in this way you can quickly open an entry box.

8. Wrong. The pencil shows that the data record is currently being edited and has not yet been saved.

9. Right. You can jump one record forward or backward or to the first or last data record.

10. Wrong, you can also record numbers, which are then treated like text. You cannot use these numbers in calculations.

11. You can sort in ascending and descending order. The icons are next to each other on the toolbar.

12. Right. Selection affects filtering.

13. No, when closed the table cancels all filters.

14. No, all numbers that can be matched with characters and special characters should be entered as Text.

15. Right. Clicking on the entry takes you directly to the Internet address.

Chapter 3

1.a. The Wizard is available immediately after start-up (or with the FILE/NEW menu command).

2.c. The style determines the background, font, and font size of all forms.

3.a. Wizards (almost) always create complete databases.

4.b. Validation rules determine what the user is allowed to enter.

5.b. Forms allow viewing of tables or queries.

6.c. Entry fields, text in the form is referred to as control elements.

7.a. Like a form, a report also displays table data.

8.b. This formula is always used when the current date is required.

9.b. The Start Overview can also be found as a form in the Form module.

10.a. Boxes control window size and display.

Chapter 4

To create a new database in the Access 2000 window, open the **File** (1) menu. You can only ever have **one** (2) database open. An open database is automatically closed, when you open or create a new database. The data records are already saved, as they are saved during **entering** (3). The Memo field can contain up to **65,535** (4) characters. As opposed to the text field, it is used for annotations and remarks. The relationships between individual tables can be found under **Relations** (5) in the **Tools** (6) menu. Forms are divided into areas. The title is usually contained in the **Header** (7), the data in the **Detail Area** (8). If you want to select more than one control element of the form, drag a frame around the elements with the **mouse** (9). The elements **do not** (10) have to be surrounded completely by the frame. To call up the properties of an element, **double-click** (11) on the element or on the *Properties* icon. The **Data Origin** property (12) shows with which table the form is linked. Reports can be found in the **Report module** (13) of the Database window. Double-clicking on a report opens it in **Print Preview** (14). The mouse pointer turns into a magnifying glass and clicking on the report **reduces** (15) it to Full Page View. A report is also divided into areas. The heading is contained in the **Header Area** (16), and the data in the **Detail Area** (17). Page numbers can always be found in the **Page Footer** (18).

Chapter 5

1. Right (for Windows 95/98 and Windows NT operating systems).

2. Wrong. It indicates that a path to a folder is going to follow.

3. Wrong. You can choose individual fields.

4. Right. You can redefine each field.

5. Right. The primary key is compulsory.

6. Wrong. The Primary Key field must be an *AutoValue* field.

7. Wrong. Call up the TOOLS/RELATIONS menu command and see for yourself.

8. Wrong. You need to double-click on the line.

9. Right. The database becomes safer with it.

10. Right. These control elements list data records from other tables.

Chapter 6

1.C. The OLE object type is used for images.

2.B. In the Form Design on the left-hand side.

3.H. The order is noticeable when entering data.

4.I. Queries collect fields from different tables.

5.E. Adds tables or field lists from tables.

6.J. It is possible to sort in ascending and descending order.

7.G. Criteria may vary in type.

8.D Apart from LIKE there are also BETWEEN, NOT, AND, and OR.

9.A. The F2 function key only opens the field.

10.F. It is also available as an option in the QUERY menu: PARAMETER.

Chapter 7

1.b. is correct. All database objects can be copied through the clipboard.

2.c. is correct. The line is created as soon as you release the mouse.

3.a. is correct. The report requires a data basis.

4.b. is correct. The style applies the correct font.

5.b. is correct. The title should be placed in the header.

6.c. is correct. Clicking on the edge selects the row.

7.a. is correct. The page number =PAGE is repeated on every page.

8.b. is correct. The field lists groups and sorting types.

9.a. is correct. Font, colours, and lines of the marked area are changed.

10.b. is correct. Labels from Avery and Hermes are available.

Chapter 8

The fields in a table structure which are linked to fields in other tables must have the **Number** field data type (1). The size of these fields is specified with **Long Integer** (2). Relationships between the tables can be viewed and modified under **Tools/Relations** (3). To create a relationship the **Primary Key field** (4) of the first table is dragged onto the linked field of the other table. With the **Delete** (5) key you can delete a selected Relationship line. You can right-align form elements with the **Format** (6) menu. Increase the vertical distance with the **Align** (7) option from this menu. A sub-form offers the data from a **different** (8) table or query for editing. When a sub-form is located in a main form you can see **two** (9) different navigation buttons. The outside arrows control the data records in the **main form** (10).

Chapter 9

1. Right. You can find it after start-up under *New Access database* or under *File/New*.

2. Wrong. The Start form can be found under Tools/Start.

3. Right. The relationship type is also displayed (usually 1:n).

4. Right. The procedure can be found in the Module sheet, the link with the button in its properties.

5. Wrong. Calculations are always created as reports.

6. Right. The group also contains the customer address.

7. Right. Excel is better for calculations in two-dimensional tables.

8. Wrong. Access is the ideal supplier for Mail Merge data.

9. Wrong. You can only use 20 characters.

10. Right. You can also divide the users into groups, create user accounts, and manage database access down to object level.

Glossary

Activation order   Determines in which order the fields of a form are activated when it is opened for data entry or editing. If the wrong field is marked after you pressed the [key you need to modify the activation order (VIEW menu).

Assistant   The Office Assistant is the funny little paperclip in a small window, which offers you its help or displays messages (if it is activated).

AutoValue   A field data type that ensures that the field is automatically calculated when a new record is added. Users cannot enter data into AutoValue fields.

ClipArt   ClipArt is images that have been produced with a computer and are stored in a computer.

Combination field   Combination fields are control elements that offer a list of data when you click on them (also: drop-down list). Combination fields can only be found in forms. They are either created by the Wizard, or directly drawn in with the corresponding tool from the Toolbox. Where data is taken from is determined by the *Data Origin* element property.

Command button   Drawing objects on forms which have as their property a link to a VBA program or a macro. When you click on the button the respective object is activated. Command buttons are drawn with a tool from the Toolbox.

Control element   Term used to refer to a field in a form or report. Control elements have properties that can be assigned and edited in Design View.

Criteria   In queries it is possible to assign criteria to individual fields. For this purpose enter the criterion in the Criteria row. The data, which is extracted by the query, will be sorted by this criterion.

Cursor   The cursor indicates where you are currently writing. When you click on an entry field with the mouse, the cursor starts flashing in the field. You can move it in this field by means of the Cursor keys.

Data access pages   A Web page in HTML format in which Access data can be displayed and edited.

Data record   A row in a table is referred to as a data record. Entries into the fields of a form and the printing of a row in the Detail area of a report are also data records.

Data Record Indicator   When you are editing a data record in a form, data sheet, or table the Data Record Indicator shows its status on the left-hand edge of the row or form. A pen means that the last change has not yet been saved, the black triangle marks already saved data records.

Data type   See ‡Field data type.

Database   A collection of objects (tables, queries, forms, reports, macros, and modules) used to store and edit data. Access is a database program.

Database window   The first and most important window of a database, which shows the individual objects distributed in modules. To switch to a different module simply click on the corresponding icon. The Database window can be activated in the Window menu.

Date   Access gets the current data from the operating system, which in turn retrieves it from the battery-operated clock of the computer. There are several Date functions (=Date(), =Month(), and so on) to integrate the date into fields, forms, or reports. You can view a list of the functions in the Editor window.

Design View   In this view the structure of a table (with field list) is edited. In this view you can see how the fields and other elements (text, lines, images) on a form or report are arranged. In the top left-hand corner there is a button to switch into Design View.

Editor   The Editor is an entry window that can be opened to edit the field properties of table fields, form fields, or report fields. For this purpose there is a small button with three dots to the right of the selected Property field. The Editor offers all the formulas and functions which can be integrated into the field.

Exclusive   Basically, databases can be edited by several users at the same time, unless you have opened them exclusively. For this purpose tick the *Exclusive* box under FILE/OPEN. Forthwith, access is denied to any other users in the network.

Field   A column in a table or the elements on a form or report that is filled with data when displayed (form) or printed out (report) is referred to as a field. Table fields have field properties, form fields and report fields possess control element properties.

Field data types   Fields must be named in the Table Design. These names are then used as column headers in the table. In the form or report the field name is less important. It can be defined through the control element properties.

Filename   The name for an amount of data (file) which is stored on a data carrier. Filenames may consist of up to 256 characters, including spaces and a few special characters. A file extension (for example, MDB for Access databases) with a dot as a separator is attached to the filename. If you cannot see these extensions you can show them with the *View/Options* menu command in Windows Explorer.

Filter   With a filter you can restrict the output, so that only part of the data contained in a table or query is shown. Filters are temporarily activated in the table sheet, Data Sheet View, or Form View. They are automatically deactivated when you close the object.

Filter by selection   A filter which uses the current selection as its criterion. For example, if the 'London' entry in the 'City' field is marked when the filter is called up, only data records which have this entry in this field are shown with hyperlinks.

Formula   A mathematical expression for the calculation of data which, apart from operators (+, -, and so on) and logical signs (> greater than, < less than, and so on), usually includes the fields of a table. Field names are written in square brackets (for example, =[Amount]*[Price]). Formulas can be used in the table structure, in queries, and in the Form/Report Design.

Function   A mathematical calculation that is offered by the program. The function =SUM([*field name*]) calculates the sum of all contents of *field name*. Functions are used in queries and in the Form and Report Design. The Editor offers a list of all functions. You can activate it with the icon with the three dots on the right-hand edge of the field you are currently editing.

Header/footer area   Forms and reports are divided into areas. The Header area usually contains the title, whereas the Footer area contains page numbers and other elements. The report differentiates between Report Header/Footer and Page Header/Footer.

Homepage   The Internet page of a company or a private person is referred to as homepage. When you call up an Internet address, as a rule the homepage is displayed first. Access can store such Internet addresses with a separate field data type (Hyperlink) in data records.

HTML   The language of the Internet. Homepages are programmed in HTML. Access stores the data access pages in HTML format.

Hyperlink   A hyperlink is a link in a data record, which calls up an Internet address. Hyperlinks can also be used in forms and reports to switch from one object to the next, you can even activate other programs such as Excel or Word.

Importing/exporting   To integrate 'external' data from other files into the database you need to import them. You may also create a dynamic link in which the original data remains in its location, or completely integrate the data. Data is exported if needed for a different database in a different file format. For example, you can export Access tables as Excel tables.

Link   See ‡Relationship.

Macro   A macro is a set of operations that are executed in Access. Access macros are small programs that open and close objects, display messages, and call up or edit data records. Macros are a timesaving alternative to VBA procedures, but not as flexible.

Module   On the one hand module is the expression used to refer to tabs in the Database window (Table module, Query module, Form module, and so on). On the other hand the term is also used to refer to a program sheet with VBA procedures, which is stored in the last *Module* module.

Navigation   This term is used to refer to moving in tables, scrolling between data records, and calling up particular data records. To navigate, the table or data sheet and the form offer suitable Arrow buttons in the Data Record Navigator (bottom left).

Object   A table, a form, and a query, as well as a report or a macro or module sheet, are objects. The Database window manages all the objects of a database.

OLE   Acronym for *Object Linking and Embedding*. The expression refers to a method of integrating parts of other alien programs into an Access window. For example, if you want a data record to contain a photograph, you need to create a field with the *OLE Object* field data type for it. When the data record is entered this field can contain the name of the OLE object (the filename of the image).

Option   Options are offered by the program. For example, when you open a menu you can choose from menu options. When you start a dialog (for example, with Tools/Options) numerous options are available to activate or deactivate on each tab.

Parameter query   A parameter is the additional piece of information that is required to carry out a query. The Parameter query requests this information before it compiles and outputs the data from the tables involved in the query. To initiate a Parameter query the question is simply written in square brackets into the Criteria row of the respective field.

Password   Apart from the user password, which you as a Windows 95/98 or NT user can enter to gain access to the operating system, a database can also be password-protected. The database is then coded and can only be opened with the correct password. You can assign a password with TOOLS/ SECURITY.

Primary key   The field in the table structure that clearly distinguishes each individual data record. The contents of the field must not be the same for any two fields. Only in this way can it be ensured that the links between the tables will work. If there is no Primary Key field when you produce a new table, Access automatically creates one.

Print   The currently edited object on your screen can be printed with the Printer icon or with File/Print. Access uses the system printer installed under Windows. It cannot offer printer installation itself. Before you actually go to print you can specify various settings (number of copies, and so on) under FILE/PRINT.

Procedure   Procedure is the term used to refer to a program which has been written in VBA (Visual Basic for Applications) and is stored in a Module sheet. Procedures are assigned to control element properties or command buttons in forms.

Projects   Access files, which permit access to SQL Server databases. In contrast to Access databases, a project does not contain data.

Property   Every element on a form or report, and every table field has its list of properties. In form fields or report fields these can be viewed in a separate window by double-clicking on them or clicking on the Properties symbol. Table field properties are displayed in the bottom half of the Design window.

Query   An instruction specifying which fields from individual tables are shown. It is also possible to include specifications as to how the fields are to be sorted and which criteria have to be fulfilled. Queries are stored in the Query module. They produce the current data from the tables when called up. Queries do not store any data.

Referential Integrity   With it Access guards the relationships between tables and ensures that data cannot be lost. If you try to delete data in a table to which another table refers, referential integrity will prevent you from doing so.

Relationship   Tables have a relationship if they are linked by shared fields. If the Supplier Number field in a Products table is linked to the Supplier Number field in the Suppliers table, the two tables have a relationship.

Report   With the help of reports the printing of data fields is designed and saved. A saved report contains no data itself but only the data layout. Only when the report is printed or viewed in Print Preview are the data from the table or query inserted.

Sorting   Tables can be sorted by individual columns (fields). First select the column and then activate the Sort icon. Sorting in ascending order first sorts the special characters and numbers and then text from A to Z.

SQL Server   A database program or database from which Access can adopt data by means of a project.

Tabs   The Database window arranges its modules on tabs. Many dialogs such as under TOOLS/OPTIONS distribute their numerous options across different tabs.

Toolbar   When you call up a database the *Database* toolbar is made available at the top edge of the program window (under the Menu bar). This toolbar displays different icons depending on what type of object is currently being edited. Many icons can only be activated if a particular element is selected. For example, you can only use the Bold symbol if a control element is selected which can be set in bold script (name or text field).

VBA   Acronym for *Visual Basic for Applications*. A programming language which is by now standardised for the Office product range. VBA programs (procedures) can be created and maintained in Module sheets in the last module of the Database window. They are activated by command buttons or properties of control elements. There are also automatic procedures, which control a database without being called up by the user. VBA programming is true object-oriented programming.

Wizards   The Access Wizards are programs that can be activated to create a table, a form, a query, or a report. They lead the user to the finished object by means of a dialog.

Word   The text-processing program from the Office product range that has a direct interface to Access tables. For example, Access tables can be transferred as Word Mail Merge source. Access data can also be exported as text files in Word format.

Zoom window   Called up with Arrow ⇧+F2, the Zoom window displays the contents of the field, which currently contains the cursor or the selection, in a large dialog field. Zoom windows facilitate the creation and modification of complex formulas in query columns, control elements, or the table structure.